Light Cooking™

❖

ENTERTAINING

PUBLICATIONS INTERNATIONAL, LTD.

Light Cooking is a trademark of Publications International, Ltd.

Food Guide Pyramid source: U.S. Department of Agriculture/U.S. Department of Health and Human Services.

Recipe Development: Jeanne Jones
Nutritional Analysis: Linda R. Yoakam, M.S., R.D.

Photography: Photo/Kevin Smith Studios, Chicago
Photographers: Doug Hunter, Kevin Smith
Photo Stylist: Lucianne Crowley
Food Stylists: Jeff Anthony, Irene Bertolucci, Teri Ernst
Assistants: Greg Shapps, Diane Soubly

Pictured on the front cover: Marinated Artichokes & Shrimp in Citrus Vinaigrette (*page 12*).
Pictured on the inside front cover: Gingered Chicken Pot Stickers (*page 22*).
Pictured on the inside back cover: Tempting Apple Trifles (*page 82*).
Pictured on the back cover (*counterclockwise from right*): Rack of Lamb with Dijon-Mustard Sauce (*page 47*), Petite Pizzas (*page 18*), Eggs Primavera (*page 48*) and Honey Carrot Cake (*page 76*).

ISBN: 0-7853-0781-8

Manufactured in U.S.A.

8 7 6 5 4 3 2 1

CONTENTS

LESSONS IN SMART EATING

Today, people everywhere are more aware than ever before about the importance of maintaining a healthful lifestyle. In addition to proper exercise, this includes eating foods that are lower in fat, sodium and cholesterol. The goal of *Light Cooking* is to provide today's cook with easy-to-prepare recipes that taste great, yet easily fit into your dietary goals. Eating well is a matter of making smarter choices about the foods you eat. Preparing the recipes in *Light Cooking* is your first step toward making smart choices a delicious reality.

A Balanced Diet

The U.S. Department of Agriculture and the Department of Health and Human Services have developed a Food Guide Pyramid to illustrate how easy it is to eat a healthier diet. It is not a rigid prescription, but rather a general guide that lets you choose a healthful diet that's right for you. It calls for eating a wide variety of foods to get the nutrients you need and, at the same time, the right amount of calories to maintain a healthy weight.

Food Guide Pyramid
A Guide to Daily Food Choices

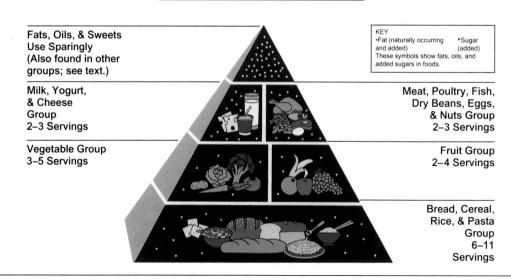

Fats, Oils, & Sweets
Use Sparingly
(Also found in other
groups; see text.)

KEY
•Fat (naturally occurring   ▾Sugar
and added)   (added)
These symbols show fats, oils, and
added sugars in foods.

Milk, Yogurt,
& Cheese
Group
2–3 Servings

Meat, Poultry, Fish,
Dry Beans, Eggs,
& Nuts Group
2–3 Servings

Vegetable Group
3–5 Servings

Fruit Group
2–4 Servings

Bread, Cereal,
Rice, & Pasta
Group
6–11
Servings

The number of servings, and consequently, the number of calories a person can eat each day, is determined by a number of factors, including age, weight, height, activity level and gender. Sedentary women and some older adults need about 1,600 calories each day. For most children, teenage girls, active women and many sedentary men 2,000 calories is about right. Teenage boys, active men and some very active women use about 2,800 calories each day. Use the chart below to determine how many servings you need for your calorie level.

Personalized Food Group Servings for Different Calorie Levels*			
	1,600	2,000	2,800
Bread Group Servings	6	8	11
Vegetable Group Servings	3	4	5
Fruit Group Servings	2	3	4
Milk Group Servings	2–3**	2–3**	2–3**
Meat Group Servings (ounces)	5	6	7

* Numbers may be rounded.
** Women who are pregnant or breast-feeding, teenagers and young adults to age 24 need 3 or more servings.

Lower Fat for Healthier Living

It is widely known that most Americans' diets are too high in fat. A low fat diet reduces your risk of getting certain diseases and helps you maintain a healthy weight. Studies have shown that eating more than the recommended amount of fat (especially saturated fat) is associated with increased blood cholesterol levels in some adults. A high blood cholesterol level is associated with increased risk for heart disease. A high fat diet may also increase your chances for obesity and some types of cancer.

Nutrition experts recommend diets that contain 30% or less of total daily calories from fat. The "30% calories from fat" goal applies to a total diet over time, not to a single food, serving of a recipe or meal. To find the approximate percentage of calories from fat use this easy 3-step process:

1 Multiply the grams of fat per serving by 9 (there are 9 calories in each gram of fat), to give you the number of calories from fat per serving.

2 Divide by the total number of calories per serving.

3 Multiply by 100%.

For example, imagine a 200 calorie sandwich that has 10 grams of fat.
To find the percentage of calories from fat, first multiply the grams of fat by 9: $10 \times 9 = 90$

Then, divide by the total number of calories in a serving: $90 \div 200 = .45$

Multiply by 100% to get the percentage of calories from fat: $45 \times 100\% = 45\%$

You may find doing all this math tiresome, so an easier way to keep track of the fat in your diet is to calculate the total *grams* of fat appropriate to your caloric intake, then keep a running count of fat grams over the course of a day. The Nutrition Reference Chart on page 92 lists recommended daily fat intakes based on calorie level.

Defining "Fat Free"

It is important to take the time to read food labels carefully. For example, you'll find many food products on the grocery store shelves making claims such as "97% fat free." This does not necessarily mean that 97% of the *calories* are free from fat (or that only 3 percent of calories come from fat). Often these numbers are calculated by weight. This means that out of 100 grams of this food, 3 grams are fat. Depending on what else is in the food, the percentage of calories from fat can be quite high. You may find that the percent of calories *from fat* can be as high as 50%.

Daily Values

Fat has become the focus of many diets and eating plans. This is because most Americans' diets are too high in fat. However, there are other important nutrients to be aware of, including saturated fat, sodium, cholesterol, protein, carbohydrates and several vitamins and minerals. Daily values for these nutrients have been established by the government and reflect current nutritional recommendations for a 2,000 calorie reference diet. They are appropriate for most adults and children (age 4 or older) and provide excellent guidelines for an overall healthy diet. The chart on page 92 gives the daily values for 11 different items.

Nutritional Analysis

Every recipe in *Light Cooking* is followed by a nutritional analysis block that lists certain nutrient values for a single serving.

■   The analysis of each recipe includes all the ingredients that are listed in that recipe, *except* ingredients labeled as "optional" or "for garnish."

■   If a range is given in the yield of a recipe ("Makes 6 to 8 servings" for example), the *lower* yield was used to calculate the per serving information.

■ If a range is offered for an ingredient ("¼ to ⅛ teaspoon" for example), the *first* amount given was used to calculate the nutrition information.

■ If an ingredient is presented with an option ("2 cups hot cooked rice or noodles" for example), the *first* item listed was used to calculate the nutritional information.

■ Foods shown in photographs on the same serving plate and offered as "serve with" suggestions at the end of a recipe are *not* included in the recipe analysis unless they are listed in the ingredient list.

■ Meat should be trimmed of all visible fat since this is reflected in the nutritional analysis.

■ In recipes calling for cooked rice or noodles, the analysis was based on rice or noodles that were prepared without added salt or fat unless otherwise mentioned in the recipe.

The nutrition information that appears with each recipe was calculated by an independent nutrition consulting firm. Every effort has been made to check the accuracy of these numbers. However, because numerous variables account for a wide range of values in certain foods, all analyses that appear in this book should be considered approximate.

The recipes in this publication are *not* intended as a medically therapeutic program, nor as a substitute for medically approved diet plans for people on fat, cholesterol or sodium restricted diets. You should consult your physician before beginning any diet plan. The recipes offered here can be a part of a healthy lifestyle that meets recognized dietary guidelines. A healthy lifestyle includes not only eating a balanced diet, but engaging in proper exercise as well.

All the ingredients called for in these recipes are generally available in large supermarkets, so there is no need to go to specialty or health food stores. You'll also see an ever-increasing amount of reduced fat and nonfat products available in local markets. Take advantage of these items to reduce your daily fat intake even more.

Cooking Healthier

When cooking great-tasting low fat meals, you will find some techniques or ingredients are different from traditional cooking. Fat serves as a flavor enhancer and gives foods a distinctive and desirable texture. In order to compensate for the lack of fat and still give great-tasting results, many of the *Light Cooking* recipes call for a selection of herbs or a combination of fresh vegetables. A wide variety of grains and pastas are also used. Many of the recipes call for alternative protein sources, such as dried beans or tofu. Often meat is included in a recipe as an accent flavor rather than the star attraction. Vegetables are often "sautéed" in a small amount of broth rather than oil. Applesauce may be added to baked goods to give a texture similar to full fat foods. These are all simple changes that you can easily make when you start cooking healthy!

APPETIZERS

CROSTINI

These tasty little Tuscan treats are colorful and easy to make. Crostini are wonderful for last minute parties or unexpected guests because they can be made in minutes.

¼ loaf whole wheat baguette (4 ounces)
4 plum tomatoes
1 cup (4 ounces) shredded part-skim mozzarella cheese
3 tablespoons prepared pesto sauce

1 Preheat oven to 400°F. Slice baguette into 16 very thin, diagonal slices. Slice each tomato vertically into four ¼-inch slices.

2 Place baguette slices on nonstick baking sheet. Top each with 1 tablespoon cheese, then 1 slice tomato. Bake about 8 minutes or until bread is lightly toasted and cheese is melted. Remove from oven; top each crostini with about ½ teaspoon pesto sauce. Garnish with fresh basil, if desired. Serve warm.   *Makes 8 appetizer servings*

Nutrients per Serving:

2 crostini

Calories	83
(34% of calories from fat)	
Total Fat	3 g
Saturated Fat	2 g
Cholesterol	9 mg
Sodium	159 mg
Carbohydrate	9 g
Dietary Fiber	<1 g
Protein	5 g
Calcium	121 mg
Iron	1 mg
Vitamin A	51 RE
Vitamin C	7 mg

DIETARY EXCHANGES:
½ Starch/Bread, ½ Lean Meat, ½ Fat

Cook's Tip
Plum tomatoes, also called Roma tomatoes, are flavorful egg-shaped tomatoes that come in red and yellow varieties. As with other tomatoes, they are very perishable. Choose firm tomatoes that are fragrant and free of blemishes. Ripe tomatoes should be stored at room temperature and used within a few days.

MARINATED ARTICHOKES & SHRIMP IN CITRUS VINAIGRETTE

Poaching the shrimp in orange juice adds a subtle and complementary flavor to the marinated artichoke hearts. This unique appetizer has only 2 grams of fat per serving and is high in vitamin C.

Nutrients per Serving:

Calories	135
(14% of calories from fat)	
Total Fat	2 g
Saturated Fat	<1 g
Cholesterol	87 mg
Sodium	236 mg
Carbohydrate	19 g
Dietary Fiber	4 g
Protein	12 g
Calcium	69 mg
Iron	2 mg
Vitamin A	66 RE
Vitamin C	61 mg

DIETARY EXCHANGES:
1 Lean Meat, 1 Fruit,
1 Vegetable

VINAIGRETTE

  1 large seedless orange, peeled and sectioned
  3 tablespoons red wine vinegar
  3 tablespoons fat free mayonnaise
  1 teaspoon fresh thyme *or* ¼ teaspoon dried thyme leaves
  2 teaspoons extra virgin olive oil

SALAD

  1 package (9 ounces) frozen artichoke hearts, thawed
12 raw shrimp (12 ounces)
  1 cup orange juice

1 To prepare vinaigrette, place all vinaigrette ingredients except oil in blender or food processor; process until smooth. Pour mixture into medium nonmetal bowl and whisk in oil until well blended. Fold artichoke hearts into vinaigrette. Cover and refrigerate several hours or overnight.

2 Peel shrimp, leaving tails attached. Devein and butterfly shrimp. Bring orange juice to a boil in medium saucepan. Add shrimp and cook about 2 minutes or *just* until they turn pink and opaque.

3 To serve, place about 3 artichoke hearts on each of 6 plates. Top each serving with 2 shrimp. Drizzle vinaigrette over tops. Garnish with fresh Italian parsley, if desired.

Makes 6 appetizer servings

ROASTED EGGPLANT SPREAD WITH FOCACCIA

This no cholesterol appetizer is perfect for any Italian meal!

Nutrients per Serving:

3 tablespoons eggplant spread with 3 wedges focaccia

Calories	127
(21% of calories from fat)	
Total Fat	3 g
Saturated Fat	<1 g
Cholesterol	0 mg
Sodium	267 mg
Carbohydrate	22 g
Dietary Fiber	3 g
Protein	4 g
Calcium	15 mg
Iron	1 mg
Vitamin A	12 RE
Vitamin C	4 mg

DIETARY EXCHANGES:
1½ Starch/Bread, ½ Fat

1 eggplant (1 pound)
1 medium tomato
1 tablespoon fresh lemon juice
1 tablespoon chopped fresh basil *or* 1 teaspoon dried basil leaves
2 teaspoons chopped fresh thyme *or* ¾ teaspoon dried thyme leaves
1 clove garlic, minced
¼ teaspoon salt
1 tablespoon extra virgin olive oil
  Focaccia (page 38)

1 Preheat oven to 400°F. Poke holes in several places in eggplant with fork. Cut stem end from tomato and place in small baking pan. Place eggplant on oven rack; bake 10 minutes. Place tomato in oven with eggplant. Bake vegetables 40 minutes.

2 Cool vegetables slightly, then peel. Cut eggplant into large slices. Place tomato and eggplant in food processor or blender. Add lemon juice, basil, thyme, garlic and salt; process until well blended. Slowly drizzle oil through feed tube and process until mixture is well blended. Refrigerate 3 hours or overnight.

3 To serve, spread 1 tablespoon on each focaccia wedge. Garnish with cherry tomato wedges and additional fresh basil, if desired. *Makes 10 appetizer servings*

Cook's Tip

When buying eggplants, look for firm eggplants with smooth skin and a uniform color. Avoid those that are soft, shriveled or have cuts or scars. Eggplants bruise easily. Handle gently and store at room temperature up to two days. Use as soon as possible since eggplants become bitter with age.

CORN AND TOMATO CHOWDER

This chowder takes advantage of the flavor of these two popular vegetables that are at their best in summer. The tomatoes are salted and drained to get rid of their water content and intensify their flavor. Most of the salt comes out during draining, adding little to the sodium content of the chowder.

1½ cups peeled and diced plum tomatoes
¾ teaspoon salt, divided
2 ears corn, husks removed
1 tablespoon margarine
½ cup finely chopped shallots
1 clove garlic, minced
1 cup chicken broth
1 can (12 ounces) evaporated skimmed milk
¼ teaspoon black pepper
1 tablespoon finely chopped fresh sage *or* 1 teaspoon rubbed sage
1 tablespoon cornstarch
2 tablespoons cold water

1 Place tomatoes in nonmetal colander over bowl. Sprinkle ½ teaspoon salt on top; toss to mix well. Allow tomatoes to drain at least 1 hour.

2 Meanwhile, cut corn kernels off the cobs into small bowl. Scrape cobs, with dull side of knife, to "milk" liquid from cobs into same bowl; set aside. Discard 1 cob; break remaining cob in half.

3 Heat margarine in heavy medium saucepan over medium-high heat until melted and bubbly. Add shallots and garlic; reduce heat to low. Cover and cook about 5 minutes or until shallots are soft and translucent. Add broth, milk, black pepper, sage and reserved corn cob halves. Bring to a boil over high heat. Reduce heat to low; simmer, uncovered, 10 minutes. Remove and discard cob halves. Add corn; return to a boil over medium-high heat. Reduce heat to low; simmer, uncovered, 15 minutes more.

4 Dissolve cornstarch in water; add to chowder, mixing well. Stir until thickened. Remove from heat; stir in drained tomatoes and remaining ¼ teaspoon salt. To serve, spoon into bowls. Garnish with additional fresh sage, if desired.

Makes 6 appetizer servings

Nutrients per Serving:

¾ cup

Calories	127
(18% of calories from fat)	
Total Fat	3 g
Saturated Fat	1 g
Cholesterol	2 mg
Sodium	430 mg
Carbohydrate	20 g
Dietary Fiber	2 g
Protein	7 g
Calcium	198 mg
Iron	1 mg
Vitamin A	315 RE
Vitamin C	14 mg

DIETARY EXCHANGES:
½ Starch/Bread, ½ Milk,
1 Vegetable, ½ Fat

PETITE PIZZAS

This recipe includes two different toppings so that you can serve only pizza at your party and still offer a variety of appetizers.

Nutrients per Serving:

2 sausage pizzas and 2 mushroom pizzas

Calories	148
(25% of calories from fat)	
Total Fat	4 g
Saturated Fat	1 g
Cholesterol	9 mg
Sodium	357 mg
Carbohydrate	22 g
Dietary Fiber	2 g
Protein	7 g
Calcium	88 mg
Iron	2 mg
Vitamin A	47 RE
Vitamin C	9 mg

DIETARY EXCHANGES:
1 Starch/Bread, ½ Lean Meat, ½ Vegetable, ½ Fat

½ cup warm water (110° to 115°F)
¾ teaspoon active dry yeast
½ teaspoon sugar
¾ cup bread flour*
¾ cup whole wheat flour
¼ teaspoon salt
1½ teaspoons extra virgin olive oil
   Pizza Sauce (page 20)
¼ cup finely chopped green bell pepper
¼ cup finely chopped onion
 2 ounces Italian turkey sausage, crumbled and cooked
⅔ cup sliced mushrooms, cooked until soft
¼ cup freshly grated Parmesan cheese
¼ cup (1 ounce) shredded part-skim mozzarella cheese

1 To prepare crust, place warm water in small bowl. Sprinkle yeast and sugar on top; stir to combine. Let stand 10 minutes or until bubbly. Combine flours and salt in medium bowl. Stir in oil and yeast mixture; mix until smooth. Knead dough on lightly floured work surface 5 minutes or until smooth and elastic. Place dough in medium bowl sprayed with nonstick cooking spray. Turn dough so top is coated with cooking spray; cover with towel. Let rise in warm place 45 minutes or until doubled in bulk. Punch down dough; place on lightly floured surface and knead 2 minutes more. Cover with towel and let rise 20 minutes more. Roll out to ¼-inch thickness and cut into 32 circles with 2-inch cookie or biscuit cutter. Place on baking sheet sprayed with cooking spray. (Combine scraps and roll out again to obtain 32 circles, if necessary.)

2 Prepare Pizza Sauce. Place about ½ teaspoon sauce on each dough round. Spread sauce gently, leaving a small border of crust.

3 Preheat oven to 400°F. Combine bell pepper and onion in small bowl. Evenly sprinkle on top of sauce. Place sausage on half the pizzas and 1 or 2 mushroom slices on each of remaining pizzas. Evenly sprinkle cheeses on pizzas. Bake 10 minutes or until cheese melts. Serve immediately. (To reheat, warm pizzas in 250°F oven 10 minutes.) Garnish with fresh basil, if desired. *Makes 8 appetizer servings*

*All-purpose flour may be substituted; however, bread flour works better with yeast since it contains more gluten. It also contains more vitamin C and potassium.

(continued on page 20)

Petite Pizzas, continued

PIZZA SAUCE

½ teaspoon extra virgin olive oil
1 clove garlic, minced
1 can (8 ounces) tomato sauce
1 tablespoon chopped fresh basil *or* 1 teaspoon dried basil leaves
½ teaspoon dried oregano leaves
Dash salt and black pepper

 Heat oil in small saucepan over medium heat. Add garlic; cook and stir 1 minute, being careful not to brown garlic. Add tomato sauce, basil and oregano; simmer 20 minutes. Stir in salt and black pepper.

CITRUS COOLER

2 cups fresh squeezed orange juice
2 cups unsweetened pineapple juice
1 teaspoon fresh lemon juice
¾ teaspoon vanilla extract
¾ teaspoon coconut extract
2 cups cold sparkling water

 Combine juices and extracts in large pitcher; refrigerate until cold. Just before serving, stir in sparkling water and pour over ice. Garnish with lemon slices, if desired.

Makes 8 servings

❖

This tropical nonalcoholic drink is refreshing and thirst quenching. It is also very high in vitamin C. This cooler is a wonderful alternative beverage for cocktail parties, and kids love it for their parties too.

❖

Nutrients per Serving:

¾ *cup*

Calories	66
(2% of calories from fat)	
Total Fat	<1 g
Saturated Fat	<1 g
Cholesterol	0 mg
Sodium	2 mg
Carbohydrate	15 g
Dietary Fiber	1 g
Protein	1 g
Calcium	25 mg
Iron	<1 mg
Vitamin A	13 RE
Vitamin C	38 mg

DIETARY EXCHANGES:
1 Fruit

GINGERED CHICKEN POT STICKERS

These Asian tidbits are also great on steamed rice as an entrée. For a meatless dish, substitute tempeh, found in Asian markets, for the chicken.

3 cups finely shredded cabbage
1 egg white, lightly beaten
1 tablespoon citrus-seasoned soy sauce or light soy sauce
¼ teaspoon crushed red pepper
1 tablespoon minced fresh ginger
4 green onions with tops, finely chopped
¼ pound ground chicken breast, cooked and drained
24 wonton wrappers, at room temperature
  Cornstarch
½ cup water
1 tablespoon oyster sauce
½ teaspoon honey
⅛ teaspoon crushed red pepper
2 teaspoons grated lemon peel
1 tablespoon peanut oil

1 Steam cabbage 5 minutes, then cool to room temperature. Squeeze out any excess moisture; set aside.

2 To prepare filling, combine egg white, soy sauce, ¼ teaspoon red pepper, ginger and green onions in large bowl; blend well. Stir in cabbage and chicken.

3 To prepare pot stickers, place 1 tablespoon filling in center of 1 wonton wrapper. Gather edges around filling, pressing firmly at top to seal. Repeat with remaining wrappers and filling. Place pot stickers on large baking sheet dusted with cornstarch. Refrigerate 1 hour or until cold.

4 Meanwhile, to prepare sauce, combine remaining ingredients except oil in small bowl; mix well. Set aside.

5 Heat oil in large nonstick skillet over high heat. Add pot stickers and cook until bottoms are golden brown. Pour sauce over top. Cover and cook 3 minutes. Uncover and cook until all liquid is absorbed. Serve warm on tray as finger food or on small plates with chopsticks as first course. *Makes 8 appetizer servings*

COLD ASPARAGUS WITH LEMON-MUSTARD DRESSING

This easy-to-make, no cholesterol first course may be served either as an appetizer at the table or with cocktails as an hors d'oeuvre. If you plan to serve it as an hors d'oeuvre, the asparagus spears may be served with the sauce separately for dipping.

12 fresh asparagus spears
2 tablespoons fat free mayonnaise
1 tablespoon sweet brown mustard
1 tablespoon fresh lemon juice
1 teaspoon grated lemon peel, divided

1 Steam asparagus until crisp-tender and bright green; immediately drain and run under cold water. Cover and refrigerate until chilled.

2 Combine mayonnaise, mustard and lemon juice in small bowl; blend well. Stir in ½ teaspoon lemon peel; set aside.

3 Divide asparagus between 2 plates. Spoon 2 tablespoons dressing over top of each serving; sprinkle each with ¼ teaspoon lemon peel. Garnish with carrot strips and edible flowers, such as pansies, violets or nasturtiums, if desired.

Makes 2 appetizer servings

Nutrients per Serving:

Calories	39
(14% of calories from fat)	
Total Fat	1 g
Saturated Fat	<1 g
Cholesterol	0 mg
Sodium	294 mg
Carbohydrate	7 g
Dietary Fiber	2 g
Protein	3 g
Calcium	33 mg
Iron	1 mg
Vitamin A	71 RE
Vitamin C	15 mg

DIETARY EXCHANGES:
1½ Vegetable

Health Note

Asparagus is a great source of glutathione, a powerful antioxidant. Studies have shown that glutathione acts against at least 30 carcinogens.

TINY SEAFOOD TOSTADAS WITH BLACK BEAN DIP

Nutrients per Serving:

4 tostadas

Calories	157
(20% of calories from fat)	
Total Fat	4 g
Saturated Fat	1 g
Cholesterol	31 mg
Sodium	747 mg
Carbohydrate	23 g
Dietary Fiber	4 g
Protein	12 g
Calcium	117 mg
Iron	1 mg
Vitamin A	148 RE
Vitamin C	21 mg

DIETARY EXCHANGES:
1 Starch/Bread, 1 Lean Meat, 1 Vegetable

❖

Nonstick cooking spray
4 (8-inch) whole wheat or flour tortillas, cut into 32 (2½-inch) rounds or other shapes
1 cup Black Bean Dip (recipe follows)
1 cup shredded fresh spinach
¾ cup tiny cooked or canned shrimp
¾ cup salsa
½ cup (2 ounces) shredded reduced fat Monterey Jack cheese
¼ cup light sour cream

1 Preheat oven to 350°F. Spray cooking spray on baking sheet. Place tortilla rounds evenly on prepared baking sheet. Lightly spray tortillas with cooking spray and bake 10 minutes. Turn over and spray again; bake 3 minutes more. Prepare Black Bean Dip.

2 To prepare tostadas, spread each toasted tortilla with 1½ teaspoons Black Bean Dip. Layer each with 1½ teaspoons shredded spinach, 1 teaspoon shrimp, 1 teaspoon salsa, a sprinkle of cheese and a dab of sour cream. Garnish with thin green chili strips or fresh cilantro, if desired. Serve immediately. *Makes 8 appetizer servings*

Nutrients per Serving:

1 tablespoon

Calories	18
(7% of calories from fat)	
Total Fat	<1 g
Saturated Fat	<1 g
Cholesterol	0 mg
Sodium	134 mg
Carbohydrate	4 g
Dietary Fiber	1 g
Protein	2 g
Calcium	3 mg
Iron	<1 mg
Vitamin A	7 RE
Vitamin C	4 mg

DIETARY EXCHANGES:
½ Starch/Bread

BLACK BEAN DIP

1 can (15 ounces) black beans, undrained
1 teaspoon chili powder
¼ teaspoon *each* salt, black pepper and ground cumin
2 drops hot pepper sauce
¾ cup minced white onion
2 cloves garlic, minced
1 can (4 ounces) chopped green chilies, drained
Corn Tortilla Chips (page 32) and raw jicama sticks (optional)

1 Drain beans, reserving 2 tablespoons liquid. Combine beans, reserved liquid, chili powder, salt, black pepper, cumin and hot pepper sauce in blender; process until smooth. Combine onion and garlic in nonstick skillet; cover and cook over low heat until onion is soft. Uncover and cook until slightly browned. Add chilies; cook 3 minutes more. Add bean mixture; mix well. Serve hot or cold with chips and jicama; garnish with pepper strips, if desired. *Makes about 24 appetizer servings*

MINTED MELON SOUP

When possible, make the mint syrup the day before you plan to make the soup. After cooling the syrup to room temperature, store it in an airtight container in the refrigerator with the mint and basil. Strain the liquid just before adding to the soup. This intensifies the subtle flavor and makes this delicious and refreshing soup even better.

1 cup water
1 tablespoon sugar
1½ cups fresh mint, including stems
2 fresh basil leaves
1½ cups diced cantaloupe
4 teaspoons fresh lemon juice, divided
1½ cups diced and seeded watermelon

1 Combine water and sugar in small saucepan; mix well. Bring to a boil over medium heat. Add mint and basil; simmer 10 minutes or until reduced by two-thirds. Remove from heat; cover and let stand at least 2 hours or until cool. Strain liquid; set aside.

 2 Place cantaloupe in blender or food processor; process until smooth. Add 2 tablespoons mint syrup and 2 teaspoons lemon juice. Blend to mix well. Pour into airtight container. Cover and refrigerate until cold. Repeat procedure with watermelon, 2 teaspoons mint syrup and remaining 2 teaspoons lemon juice. Discard any remaining mint syrup.

 3 To serve, simultaneously pour ¼ cup of each melon soup, side by side, into a serving bowl. Place 1 mint sprig in center for garnish, if desired. Repeat with remaining soup.

Makes 4 appetizer servings

Nutrients per Serving:

Calories	48
(7% of calories from fat)	
Total Fat	<1 g
Saturated Fat	0 g
Cholesterol	0 mg
Sodium	7 mg
Carbohydrate	11 g
Dietary Fiber	1 g
Protein	1 g
Calcium	12 mg
Iron	<1 mg
Vitamin A	216 RE
Vitamin C	33 mg

DIETARY EXCHANGES:
1 Fruit

❖

Entertaining Tip

Select the entrée first, then plan the other dishes around it. Pick foods with a variety of color, texture and contrasting flavors for good eye and taste appeal. A monochromatic meal is not only visually uninteresting, but is usually perceived as less flavorful.

❖

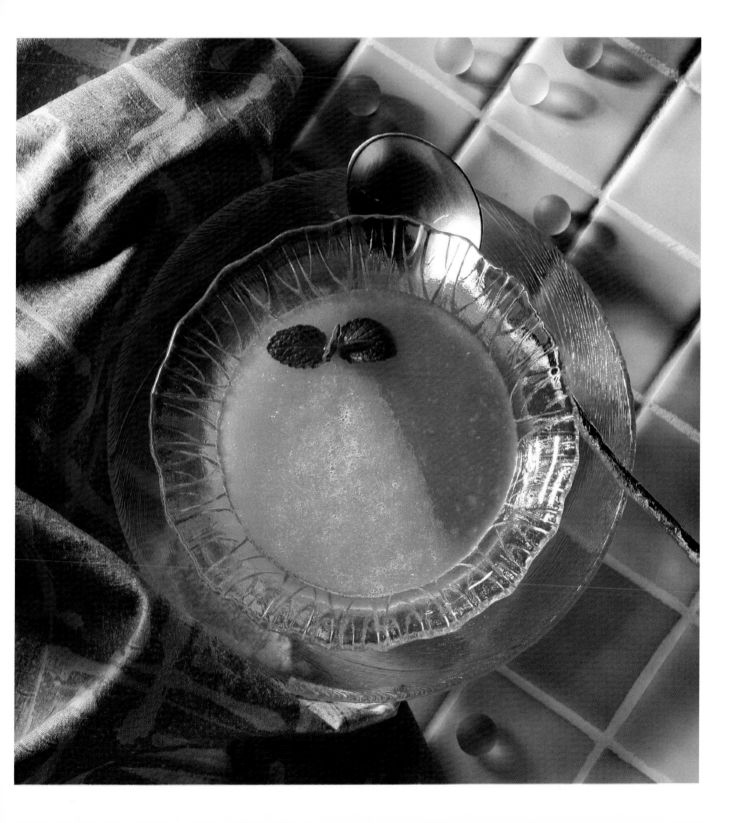

POLENTA TRIANGLES

This recipe uses corn grits rather than cornmeal because corn grits give the polenta a heartier texture. Yellow grits have a nice golden color; however, white corn grits are more readily available and may be substituted. You can find grits in most supermarket cereal aisles.

½ cup yellow corn grits
1½ cups chicken broth, divided
2 cloves garlic, minced
½ cup (2 ounces) crumbled feta cheese
1 red bell pepper, roasted,* peeled and finely chopped
Nonstick cooking spray

1 Combine grits and ½ cup broth; mix well and set aside. Pour remaining 1 cup broth into heavy large saucepan; bring to a boil. Add garlic and moistened grits; mix well and return to a boil. Reduce heat to low; cover and cook 20 minutes. Remove from heat; add feta cheese. Stir until cheese is completely melted. Add red pepper; mix well.

2 Spray 8-inch square pan with cooking spray. Spoon grits mixture into prepared pan. Press grits evenly into pan with wet fingertips. Refrigerate until cold.

3 Preheat broiler. Turn polenta out onto cutting board and cut into 2-inch squares. Cut each square diagonally into 2 triangles. Spray baking sheet with cooking spray. Place polenta triangles on prepared baking sheet and spray tops lightly with cooking spray. Place under broiler until lightly browned. Turn triangles over and broil until browned and crisp. Serve warm or at room temperature. Garnish with fresh oregano and chives, if desired. *Makes 8 appetizer servings*

*Place pepper on foil-lined broiler pan; broil 15 minutes or until blackened on all sides, turning every 5 minutes. Place pepper in paper bag; close bag and let stand 15 minutes before peeling.

Nutrients per Serving:

6 triangles

Calories	62
(26% of calories from fat)	
Total Fat	2 g
Saturated Fat	1 g
Cholesterol	6 mg
Sodium	142 mg
Carbohydrate	9 g
Dietary Fiber	<1 g
Protein	3 g
Calcium	37 mg
Iron	1 mg
Vitamin A	26 RE
Vitamin C	7 mg

DIETARY EXCHANGES:
1 Starch/Bread

SPICED APPLE TEA

2 cups unsweetened apple juice
6 whole cloves
1 cinnamon stick
3 cups water
3 bags cinnamon herbal tea

1 Combine juice, cloves and cinnamon stick in small saucepan. Bring to a boil over high heat. Reduce heat to low; simmer 10 minutes.

2 Meanwhile, place water in medium saucepan. Bring to a boil over high heat. Remove from heat; drop in tea bags and allow to steep for 6 minutes. Remove and discard tea bags.

3 Strain juice mixture; discard spices. Stir juice mixture into tea. Serve warm with additional cinnamon sticks, if desired *or* refrigerate and serve cold over ice. (Tea may be made ahead and reheated.)

Makes 4 servings

Nutrients per Serving:

about 1 cup

Calories	55
(0% of calories from fat)	
Total Fat	0 g
Saturated Fat	0 g
Cholesterol	0 mg
Sodium	5 mg
Carbohydrate	14 g
Dietary Fiber	<1 g
Protein	0 g
Calcium	4 mg
Iron	1 mg
Vitamin A	0 RE
Vitamin C	0 mg

DIETARY EXCHANGES:
1 Fruit

CORN TORTILLA CHIPS

6 corn tortillas
  Nonstick cooking spray
½ teaspoon dried oregano leaves
¼ teaspoon ground cumin

1 Preheat oven to 400°F. Cut each tortilla into 6 triangles with pizza cutter or sharp knife. Place on baking sheet in a single layer.

2 Spray tortilla triangles lightly with cooking spray and quickly sprinkle evenly with oregano and cumin.

3 Immediately bake 5 to 10 minutes until edges are golden brown and chips are crispy. (Do not make these the day before serving; they will become soft if they sit too long.)

Makes 6 appetizer servings

Note: Recipe pictured on pages 27 and 59.

Nutrients per Serving:

6 chips

Calories	57
(10% of calories from fat)	
Total Fat	1 g
Saturated Fat	<1 g
Cholesterol	0 mg
Sodium	40 mg
Carbohydrate	12 g
Dietary Fiber	0 g
Protein	1 g
Calcium	47 mg
Iron	<1 mg
Vitamin A	1 RE
Vitamin C	<1 mg

DIETARY EXCHANGES:
1 Starch/Bread

BREADS

MINIATURE FRUIT MUFFINS

These high fiber, nearly fat free muffins are just as delicious as they are appealing in appearance. Dividing the basic batter into thirds allows you to offer your guests three choices.

Nutrients per Serving:

3 miniature muffins (1 blueberry, 1 banana, 1 applesauce raisin)

Calories	130
(4% of calories from fat)	
Total Fat	1 g
Saturated Fat	<1 g
Cholesterol	1 mg
Sodium	178 mg
Carbohydrate	29 g
Dietary Fiber	2 g
Protein	3 g
Calcium	49 mg
Iron	1 mg
Vitamin A	4 RE
Vitamin C	2 mg

DIETARY EXCHANGES:
1 Starch/Bread, 1 Fruit

1 cup whole wheat flour
¾ cup all-purpose flour
½ cup firmly packed dark brown sugar
2 teaspoons baking powder
½ teaspoon baking soda
¼ teaspoon salt
1 cup buttermilk, divided
¾ cup frozen blueberries
1 small ripe banana, mashed
¼ teaspoon vanilla extract
⅓ cup unsweetened applesauce
2 tablespoons raisins
½ teaspoon ground cinnamon

1 Preheat oven to 400°F. Spray 36 miniature muffin cups with nonstick cooking spray.

2 Combine flours, brown sugar, baking powder, baking soda and salt in medium bowl. Place ⅔ cup dry ingredients in each of 2 small bowls.

3 To one portion of flour mixture, add ⅓ cup buttermilk and blueberries. Stir just until blended; spoon into 12 prepared muffin cups. To second portion, add ⅓ cup buttermilk, banana and vanilla. Stir just until blended; spoon into 12 muffin cups. To final portion, add remaining ⅓ cup buttermilk, applesauce, raisins and cinnamon. Stir just until blended; spoon into 12 muffin cups.

4 Bake 18 minutes or until lightly browned and wooden pick inserted into centers comes out clean. Cool slightly before serving. *Makes 12 servings*

WHOLE WHEAT HERB BREAD

⅔ cup water
⅔ cup skim milk
2 teaspoons sugar
2 envelopes active dry yeast
3 egg whites, lightly beaten
3 tablespoons olive oil
1 teaspoon salt
½ teaspoon *each* dried basil leaves and dried oregano leaves
4 to 4½ cups whole wheat flour

1 Bring water to a boil in small saucepan. Remove from heat; stir in milk and sugar. When mixture is warm (110° to 115°F), add yeast. (Water at higher temperatures will kill the yeast.) Mix well; let stand 10 minutes or until bubbly.

2 Combine egg whites, oil, salt, basil and oregano in large bowl until well blended. Add yeast mixture; mix well. Add 4 cups flour, ½ cup at a time, mixing well after each addition, until dough is no longer sticky. Knead about 5 minutes or until smooth and elastic, adding more flour if dough is sticky. Form into a ball. Cover and let rise in warm place about 1 hour or until doubled in bulk.

3 Preheat oven to 350°F. Punch dough down and place on lightly floured surface. Divide into 4 pieces and roll each piece into a ball. Lightly spray baking sheet with nonstick cooking spray. Place dough balls on prepared baking sheet. Bake 30 to 35 minutes until golden brown and loaves sound hollow when tapped with finger.

Makes 24 slices

Nutrients per Serving:

1 slice

Calories	99
(18% of calories from fat)	
Total Fat	2 g
Saturated Fat	<1 g
Cholesterol	<1 mg
Sodium	101 mg
Carbohydrate	17 g
Dietary Fiber	3 g
Protein	4 g
Calcium	18 mg
Iron	1 mg
Vitamin A	5 RE
Vitamin C	<1 mg

DIETARY EXCHANGES:
1 Starch/Bread, ½ Fat

APRICOT BUTTER

1 cup dried apricots (5 ounces)
1 cup unsweetened apple juice

1 Combine apricots and juice in small saucepan; bring to a boil over medium-high heat. Reduce heat to low; cover and simmer 20 minutes, stirring occasionally. Remove from heat; cool slightly. Pour mixture into blender or food processor; process until smooth. Cool to room temperature and refrigerate in airtight container or jar with tight fitting lid up to 3 months.

Makes 16 servings

Nutrients per Serving:

1 tablespoon

Calories	28
(1% of calories from fat)	
Total Fat	<1 g
Saturated Fat	<1 g
Cholesterol	0 mg
Sodium	1 mg
Carbohydrate	7 g
Dietary Fiber	1 g
Protein	<1 g
Calcium	4 mg
Iron	<1 mg
Vitamin A	64 RE
Vitamin C	<1 mg

DIETARY EXCHANGES:
½ Fruit

FOCACCIA

This focaccia is made into three small rounds rather than one large round so it may be cut into small pie-shaped wedges for spreading or dipping as an appetizer. This recipe calls for whole wheat flour to increase the fiber content. Recipe pictured on page 15.

Nutrients per Serving:

3 wedges

Calories	102
(15% of calories from fat)	
Total Fat	2 g
Saturated Fat	<1 g
Cholesterol	0 mg
Sodium	214 mg
Carbohydrate	19 g
Dietary Fiber	2 g
Protein	3 g
Calcium	9 mg
Iron	1 mg
Vitamin A	<1 RE
Vitamin C	<1 mg

DIETARY EXCHANGES:
1½ Starch/Bread

¾ cup warm water (110° to 115°F)*
1½ teaspoons sugar
  1 teaspoon active dry yeast
  1 tablespoon extra virgin olive oil
  1 teaspoon salt
  1 teaspoon dried rosemary
  1 cup all-purpose flour
  1 cup whole wheat flour
    Nonstick cooking spray

1 Pour water into large bowl. Dissolve sugar and yeast in water; let stand 10 minutes or until bubbly. Stir in oil, salt and rosemary. Add flours, ½ cup at a time, stirring until dough begins to pull away from side of bowl and forms a ball.

2 Turn dough onto lightly floured surface and knead 5 minutes or until dough is smooth and elastic, adding more flour if necessary. Place dough in bowl lightly sprayed with cooking spray and turn dough so all sides are coated. Cover with towel or plastic wrap and let rise in warm draft-free place about 1 hour or until doubled in bulk.

3 Turn dough onto lightly floured surface and knead 1 minute. Divide into 3 balls; roll each into 6-inch circle. Using fingertips, dimple surfaces of dough. Place on baking sheet sprayed with cooking spray; cover and let rise 30 minutes more.

4 Preheat oven to 400°F. Spray tops of dough circles with cooking spray; bake about 13 minutes or until golden brown. Remove from oven and cut each loaf into 10 wedges.

Makes 10 servings

*Water at higher temperatures will kill the yeast.

GARLIC BREAD

Both the taste and texture of good sourdough bread are perfect for this savory hot bread. Adding just a small amount of extra virgin olive oil to the roasted garlic prevents the bread from getting dry. Recipe pictured on page 51.

Nutrients per Serving:

1 piece

Calories	149
(16% of calories from fat)	
Total Fat	3 g
Saturated Fat	<1 g
Cholesterol	0 mg
Sodium	261 mg
Carbohydrate	27 g
Dietary Fiber	<1 g
Protein	5 g
Calcium	58 mg
Iron	1 mg
Vitamin A	1 RE
Vitamin C	4 mg

DIETARY EXCHANGES:
1½ Starch/Bread,
1 Vegetable, ½ Fat

---

6 whole heads of garlic
1 teaspoon dried oregano leaves
4½ teaspoons extra virgin olive oil
1 loaf, unsliced, crusty sourdough or French bread, cut horizontally in half (1½ pounds)
Black pepper

1 Preheat oven to 350°F. Cut tops off heads of garlic and peel each head. Place heads, cut sides up, in small baking pan and sprinkle with oregano. Cover tightly with foil and bake 30 minutes. Uncover and bake 30 minutes more. Remove from oven; cool until easy to handle.

2 Carefully squeeze soft roasted garlic out of each clove to yield about ¾ cup. Place in blender or food processor; add oil and process until smooth.

3 Spread garlic mixture evenly on both halves of bread and sprinkle lightly with black pepper. Place halves together and cut loaf vertically into 8 equal pieces, being careful to keep loaf intact. Wrap tightly in foil. Bake 30 minutes.

4 To serve, unwrap loaf leaving foil crushed around outside to keep warm.

Makes 16 servings

Health Note
Garlic has been shown to lower blood-cholesterol levels and also contains multiple antioxidants and immune-system boosters. Garlic also acts as an effective decongestant and anti-inflammatory agent, making it a good cold medication. Some studies have even shown that garlic can kill bacteria, acting as an antibiotic.

ROSEMARY BREAD STICKS

These amusing looking and low fat bread sticks are real conversation pieces as well as being simply delicious. They are also so easy to make that you may find them a fun addition to many menus. Try other herb and spice variations, such as thyme or cumin, in place of the rosemary.

⅔ cup 2% low fat milk
¼ cup finely chopped fresh chives
2 teaspoons baking powder
1 teaspoon finely chopped fresh rosemary or dried rosemary
¾ teaspoon salt
½ teaspoon black pepper
¾ cup whole wheat flour
¾ cup all-purpose flour
Nonstick cooking spray

1 Combine milk, chives, baking powder, rosemary, salt and black pepper in large bowl; mix well. Stir in flours, ½ cup at a time, until blended. Turn onto floured surface and knead dough about 5 minutes or until smooth and elastic, adding a little more flour if dough is sticky. Let stand 30 minutes at room temperature.

2 Preheat oven to 375°F. Spray baking sheet with cooking spray.

3 Divide dough into 12 equal balls, about 1¼ ounces each. Roll each ball into long thin rope and place on prepared baking sheet. Lightly spray bread sticks with cooking spray.

4 Bake about 12 minutes or until bottoms are golden brown. Turn bread sticks over and bake about 10 minutes more or until other side is browned.

Makes 12 bread sticks

Nutrients per Serving:

1 bread stick

Calories	62
(7% of calories from fat)	
Total Fat	1 g
Saturated Fat	<1 g
Cholesterol	1 mg
Sodium	196 mg
Carbohydrate	12 g
Dietary Fiber	1 g
Protein	2 g
Calcium	33 mg
Iron	1 mg
Vitamin A	13 RE
Vitamin C	1 mg

DIETARY EXCHANGES:
1 Starch/Bread

Entertaining Tip

Not every item on the menu needs to be a showstopper. Select one or two involved recipes and let the remainder be store-bought or easy to make ahead. Many guests like to bring a dessert or appetizer. Be sure to have some ideas ready so you may offer suggestions that complement the meal.

ENTREES

VEGETABLE RISOTTO

2 cups broccoli flowerets
1 cup finely chopped zucchini
1 cup finely chopped yellow squash
1 cup finely chopped red bell pepper
2½ cups chicken broth
1 tablespoon extra virgin olive oil
2 tablespoons finely chopped onion
½ cup Arborio or other short-grain rice
¼ cup dry white wine or water
⅓ cup freshly grated Parmesan cheese

1 Steam broccoli, zucchini, yellow squash and bell pepper 3 minutes or just until crisp-tender. Rinse with cold water; drain and set aside.

2 Bring broth to a simmer in small saucepan; keep hot on low heat.

3 Heat oil in heavy large saucepan over medium-high heat until hot. Add onion; reduce heat to medium. Cook and stir about 5 minutes or until onion is translucent. Add rice, stirring to coat with oil. Add wine; cook and stir until almost dry. Add ½ cup hot broth; cook and stir until broth is absorbed. Continue adding broth, ½ cup at a time, allowing broth to absorb before each addition and stirring frequently. (Total cooking time for broth absorption is about 20 minutes.)

4 Remove from heat and stir in cheese. Add steamed vegetables and mix well. Serve immediately.

Makes 6 servings

This tasty Italian rice dish contains almost no cholesterol since it is made with olive oil instead of butter.

Nutrients per Serving:

Calories	150
(27% of calories from fat)	
Total Fat	5 g
Saturated Fat	1 g
Cholesterol	4 mg
Sodium	253 mg
Carbohydrate	20 g
Dietary Fiber	2 g
Protein	7 g
Calcium	107 mg
Iron	2 mg
Vitamin A	93 RE
Vitamin C	59 mg

DIETARY EXCHANGES:
1 Starch/Bread,
1 Vegetable, 1 Fat

SALMON EN PAPILLOTE

To eliminate last minute clean up before your guest arrives, prepare this dish in advance and refrigerate until you are ready to cook. The Dilled Wine Sauce may either be spooned into the package when you open it or served on the side.

¾ cup water
1 teaspoon extra virgin olive oil
¼ teaspoon salt
⅛ teaspoon black pepper
½ cup couscous
  Parchment paper
1 small yellow squash, cut into julienned strips (1 cup)
½ pound fresh salmon fillet, bones removed and cut into 2 pieces
½ cup peeled and diced plum tomatoes
2 teaspoons *each* chopped fresh dill and chopped fresh tarragon *or*
  ¼ teaspoon *each* dried dill weed and dried tarragon leaves
2 teaspoons *each* chopped fresh chives and chopped fresh parsley
1 egg, beaten
  Dilled Wine Sauce (page 46)

1 Preheat oven to 350°F. To prepare couscous, combine water, oil, salt and black pepper in small saucepan with tight fitting lid. Bring to a boil. Add couscous and mix well. Cover and remove from heat. Let stand 5 minutes or until all liquid is absorbed.

2 Make 2 large hearts with 2 sheets parchment paper by folding each piece in half and cutting into half-heart shape. Unfold hearts and spoon ½ cup couscous on one side of each heart. Top each with ½ cup squash, 1 piece salmon, ¼ cup tomato and 1 teaspoon *each* dill, tarragon, chives and parsley. To seal packages, brush outer edges of hearts with beaten egg. Fold over again making half-heart shapes; press edges together, crimping tightly with fingers. Place packages on ungreased baking sheet; bake 14 minutes. Meanwhile, prepare Dilled Wine Sauce.

3 To serve, place each package on large plate and cut an "X" in top. Fold corners back and drizzle sauce over each serving. Garnish with edible flowers, such as pansies, violets or nasturtiums, if desired.

Makes 2 servings

(continued on page 46)

Salmon en Papillote, continued

Nutrients per Serving:	
includes ¼ cup sauce	
Calories	497
(26% of calories from fat)	
Total Fat	14 g
Saturated Fat	3 g
Cholesterol	127 mg
Sodium	387 mg
Carbohydrate	54 g
Dietary Fiber	11 g
Protein	29 g
Calcium	131 mg
Iron	4 mg
Vitamin A	146 RE
Vitamin C	24 mg

DIETARY EXCHANGES:
3 Starch/Bread, 3 Lean
Meat, 2 Vegetable, 1½ Fat

DILLED WINE SAUCE

  1½ cups finely chopped onions
    1 tablespoon dried dill weed *or* ½ cup chopped fresh dill
  1½ teaspoons dried tarragon leaves *or* ¼ cup chopped fresh tarragon
    1 clove garlic, peeled and quartered
    ½ cup dry white wine
    2 teaspoons extra virgin olive oil

 Combine all ingredients except oil in blender or food processor; process until smooth.

 Pour dill mixture into small saucepan and bring to a boil over medium heat. Reduce heat to low; simmer until reduced by half. Strain sauce into small bowl, pressing all liquid through strainer with back of spoon. Slowly whisk in oil until smooth and well blended.
Makes ½ cup

❖

Entertaining Tip

Review the recipes you plan to make, then prepare a
comprehensive grocery list. Last minute dashes to the
supermarket can be very stressful.

❖

RACK OF LAMB WITH DIJON-MUSTARD SAUCE

If you prefer really rare lamb turn the oven off after just 5 minutes, or if you like your lamb well done leave the oven on for 10 to 12 minutes. You may leave the lamb in the oven for more than 30 minutes; what is crucial is that you turn off the oven at the correct time. This allows the host or hostess more time with the guests. Recipe pictured on page 41.

1 rack of lamb (3 pounds), all visible fat removed
1 cup finely chopped fresh parsley
½ cup Dijon-style mustard
½ cup soft whole wheat bread crumbs
1 tablespoon chopped fresh rosemary *or* 2 teaspoons dried rosemary
1 teaspoon minced garlic
Rosemary Bread Sticks (page 40)

1 Preheat oven to 500°F. Place lamb in large baking pan.

2 Combine parsley, mustard, bread crumbs, rosemary and garlic in small bowl. Spread evenly over top of lamb. Place in center of oven; cook 7 minutes for medium-rare. *Turn off oven but do not open door for at least 30 minutes.*

3 Serve 2 to 3 chops on each plate, depending on size and total number of chops. Serve with Rosemary Bread Sticks. Garnish with additional fresh rosemary, lemon slices and lemon peel strips, if desired. *Makes 6 servings*

Nutrients per Serving:

4 ounces lamb with 2 bread sticks

Calories	437
(37% of calories from fat)	
Total Fat	18 g
Saturated Fat	6 g
Cholesterol	111 mg
Sodium	790 mg
Carbohydrate	28 g
Dietary Fiber	3 g
Protein	40 g
Calcium	131 mg
Iron	5 mg
Vitamin A	71 RE
Vitamin C	14 mg

DIETARY EXCHANGES:
2 Starch/Bread, 4 Lean Meat, 1½ Fat

Entertaining Tip

Do not invite more people than you can comfortably seat at your table. Guests may become uncomfortable if the table is crowded. Also, make sure you have enough serving dishes and utensils.

EGGS PRIMAVERA

The bread bowls make an elegant and unusual presentation for these tasty eggs. This dish may also be served by itself accompanied by a basket of rolls and an assortment of fresh fruit for another wonderful brunch menu.

Nutrients per Serving:

*¼ egg mixture with
1 ounce of bread*

Calories	201
(26% of calories from fat)	
Total Fat	6 g
Saturated Fat	2 g
Cholesterol	114 mg
Sodium	336 mg
Carbohydrate	23 g
Dietary Fiber	4 g
Protein	14 g
Calcium	170 mg
Iron	2 mg
Vitamin A	116 RE
Vitamin C	46 mg

DIETARY EXCHANGES:
1 Starch/Bread, 1½ Lean
Meat, 1 Vegetable, ½ Fat

---

4 round loaves (4 inches) Whole Wheat Herb Bread (page 36)*
   Nonstick cooking spray
1½ cups chopped onions
¾ cup chopped yellow squash
¾ cup chopped zucchini
½ cup chopped red bell pepper
2 ounces snow peas, trimmed and cut into thirds diagonally
¼ cup finely chopped fresh parsley
1½ teaspoons finely chopped fresh thyme *or* ¾ teaspoon dried thyme leaves
1 teaspoon finely chopped fresh rosemary *or* ½ teaspoon dried rosemary
2 whole eggs
4 egg whites
¼ teaspoon black pepper
½ cup (2 ounces) shredded reduced fat Swiss cheese

1 Preheat oven to 350°F. Slice top off each loaf of bread. Carefully hollow out each loaf, leaving walls ½ inch thick. Reserve centers for another use, such as croutons or bread crumbs. Place loaves and tops, cut sides up, on baking sheet. Spray all surfaces with cooking spray; bake 15 minutes or until well toasted.

2 Meanwhile, spray large nonstick skillet with cooking spray and heat over medium heat until hot. Add onions; cook and stir 3 minutes or until soft. Add yellow squash, zucchini and bell pepper; cook and stir 3 minutes or until crisp-tender. Add snow peas, parsley, thyme and rosemary; cook and stir 1 minute. Whisk whole eggs, egg whites and black pepper in small bowl until blended. Add to vegetable mixture; gently stir until eggs begin to set. Sprinkle cheese over top; gently stir until cheese melts and eggs are set but not dry.

3 Fill each bread bowl with ¼ of egg filling mixture, about 1 cup. Place tops back on bread bowls off center so filling shows. Place on serving plates.   *Makes 4 servings*

*Bread bowls are optional. Omit step 1, if desired, and divide eggs among 4 serving plates and serve with desired bread or rolls.

GRILLED MARINATED CHICKEN

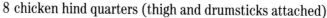

Although dark meat has more fat than white meat, removing the skin before grilling eliminates a lot of the fat. By marinating the chicken overnight in this tasty fat free marinade, the chicken stays moist even without the skin.

8 chicken hind quarters (thigh and drumsticks attached)
6 ounces frozen lemonade concentrate, thawed
2 tablespoons white wine vinegar
1 tablespoon grated lemon peel
2 cloves garlic, minced
  Garlic Bread (page 39)

1 Remove skin and all visible fat from chicken. Place chicken in 13×9-inch glass baking dish. Combine all remaining ingredients except Garlic Bread in small bowl, blending well. Pour over chicken. Cover and refrigerate 3 hours or overnight, turning chicken occasionally.

2 Lightly coat grid of grill with vegetable cooking spray. Heat grill until coals are glowing. Place chicken on grill and cook 10 to 15 minutes per side or until juices run clear when pierced with fork and chicken is no longer pink near bone. (Do not overcook or chicken will be dry.) Serve with Garlic Bread. Garnish with curly endive and lemon peel strips, if desired.

Makes 8 servings

Nutrients per Serving:

1 chicken quarter with 2 pieces Garlic Bread

Calories	518
(28% of calories from fat)	
Total Fat	16 g
Saturated Fat	4 g
Cholesterol	93 mg
Sodium	609 mg
Carbohydrate	57 g
Dietary Fiber	1 g
Protein	35 g
Calcium	129 mg
Iron	4 mg
Vitamin A	21 RE
Vitamin C	11 mg

DIETARY EXCHANGES:
4 Starch/Bread, 3½ Lean Meat, ½ Vegetable, ½ Fat

Cook's Tip

To easily peel garlic, place a clove on a cutting board. Cover the clove with the flat side of a chef's knife blade, then firmly press down on the blade with your fist. This loosens the skin so that it comes right off.

CHEDDAR CHEESE STRATA

This make-ahead marvel is perfect for entertaining. You may make it the night before and have your entrée ready in just one hour the day of your party.

1 pound French bread, cut into ½- to ¾-inch slices, crusts removed, divided
2 cups (8 ounces) shredded reduced fat Cheddar cheese, divided
2 whole eggs
3 egg whites
1 quart skim milk
1 teaspoon grated fresh onion
1 teaspoon dry mustard
½ teaspoon salt
  Paprika to taste

1 Spray 13×9-inch glass baking dish with nonstick cooking spray. Place half the bread slices in bottom of prepared dish, overlapping slightly if necessary. Sprinkle with 1¼ cups cheese. Place remaining bread slices on top of cheese.

2 Whisk whole eggs and egg whites in large bowl. Add milk, onion, mustard and salt; whisk until well blended. Pour evenly over bread and cheese. Cover with remaining ¾ cup cheese and sprinkle with paprika. Cover and refrigerate 1 hour or overnight.

3 Preheat oven to 350°F. Bake strata about 45 minutes or until cheese is melted and bread is golden brown. Let stand 5 minutes before serving. Garnish with red bell pepper stars and fresh Italian parsley, if desired. *Makes 8 servings*

Nutrients per Serving:

Calories	297
(23% of calories from fat)	
Total Fat	7 g
Saturated Fat	3 g
Cholesterol	70 mg
Sodium	962 mg
Carbohydrate	38 g
Dietary Fiber	<1 g
Protein	18 g
Calcium	406 mg
Iron	143 mg
Vitamin A	160 RE
Vitamin C	1 mg

DIETARY EXCHANGES:
2 Starch/Bread, 1 Lean Meat, ½ Milk, 1 Fat

Health Note

To eliminate 53 mg of cholesterol per serving in this recipe, you may replace the whole eggs and egg whites with 1 cup egg substitute.

SEAFOOD PAELLA

Paella is considered the national dish of Spain, but varies from one region to another depending on the ingredients available. This version is most prevalent along the Spanish coast.

Nutrients per Serving:

Calories	357
(9% of calories from fat)	
Total Fat	4 g
Saturated Fat	1 g
Cholesterol	98 mg
Sodium	281 mg
Carbohydrate	46 g
Dietary Fiber	3 g
Protein	27 g
Calcium	99 mg
Iron	6 mg
Vitamin A	90 RE
Vitamin C	43 mg

DIETARY EXCHANGES:
2½ Starch/Bread, 2 Lean Meat, 2½ Vegetable

1 tablespoon olive oil
4 cloves garlic, minced
4½ cups finely chopped onions
2 cups uncooked long-grain white rice
2 cups clam juice
2 cups dry white wine
3 tablespoons fresh lemon juice
½ teaspoon paprika
½ teaspoon saffron or ground turmeric
¼ cup boiling water
1½ cups peeled and diced plum tomatoes
½ cup finely chopped fresh parsley
1 jar (8 ounces) roasted red peppers, drained, thinly sliced and divided
1 pound bay scallops, rinsed and drained
1½ cups frozen peas, thawed
10 clams, scrubbed
10 mussels, scrubbed
20 large shrimp (1 pound), shelled and deveined

1 Preheat oven to 375°F. Heat oil in large ovenproof skillet or paella pan over medium-low heat until hot. Add garlic and cook just until garlic sizzles. Add onions and rice; cook and stir 10 minutes or until onions are soft. Stir in clam juice, wine, lemon juice and paprika; mix well.

2 Combine saffron and boiling water in small bowl; stir until saffron is dissolved. Stir into onion mixture. Stir in tomatoes, parsley and half the red pepper. Bring to a boil over medium heat. Remove from heat; cover. Place on lowest shelf of oven. Bake 1 hour or until all liquid is absorbed.

3 Remove from oven; stir in scallops and peas. *Turn oven off;* return paella to oven. Steam clams and mussels 4 to 6 minutes, removing each as shells open. Discard any unopened clams or mussels. Steam shrimp 2 to 3 minutes *just* until shrimp turn pink and opaque.

4 To serve, remove paella from oven and arrange clams, mussels and shrimp on top. Garnish with remaining red pepper.

Makes 10 servings

SOUTHWESTERN BEEF AND BEAN LASAGNA

❖

This delicate one-dish meal is packed with protein from beans and lean beef without all the fat, so there's no need to skimp on the serving size. However, for lighter appetites and children, this variation to the Italian classic may easily be stretched to 10 servings.

❖

Nutrients per Serving:

Calories	416
(25% of calories from fat)	
Total Fat	12 g
Saturated Fat	4 g
Cholesterol	40 mg
Sodium	1270 mg
Carbohydrate	50 g
Dietary Fiber	5 g
Protein	30 g
Calcium	271 mg
Iron	3 mg
Vitamin A	262 RE
Vitamin C	36 mg

DIETARY EXCHANGES:
2½ Starch/Bread, 2 Lean Meat, 3 Vegetable, 1 Fat

½ pound extra lean ground beef
1 can (16 ounces) pinto beans, drained
1 teaspoon cumin seeds *or* ½ teaspoon ground cumin
1 teaspoon olive oil
1½ cups chopped onions
1 tablespoon seeded and minced jalapeño pepper
1 clove garlic, minced
4 cups no-salt-added tomato sauce
1 can (4 ounces) diced green chilies, undrained
2 teaspoons chili powder
1 teaspoon dried oregano leaves
1 container (8 ounces) nonfat cottage cheese
1½ cups (6 ounces) shredded reduced fat Cheddar cheese, divided
1 egg white
¼ cup chopped fresh cilantro
½ teaspoon salt
¼ teaspoon black pepper
8 ounces uncooked lasagna noodles
1 cup water

 Brown beef in large skillet. Drain off fat. Stir in beans; set aside. Place cumin seeds in large nonstick skillet. Cook and stir over medium heat 2 minutes or until fragrant (omit step if using ground). Remove from skillet. In same skillet, heat oil. Add onions, jalapeño and garlic; cook until onions are soft. Add tomato sauce, green chilies, chili powder, oregano and roasted cumin seeds or ground cumin. Bring to a boil; reduce heat. Simmer, uncovered, 20 minutes.

 Preheat oven to 350°F. Combine cottage cheese, ½ cup Cheddar cheese, egg white, cilantro, salt and black pepper in medium bowl. Spray 13×9-inch baking pan with nonstick cooking spray. Cover bottom with ¾ cup tomato sauce mixture. Place layer of noodles on sauce. Spread half the beef mixture over noodles, then place another layer of noodles on top. Spread cheese mixture over noodles. Spread with remaining beef mixture. Layer with noodles. Pour remaining sauce mixture over all; sprinkle with remaining 1 cup Cheddar cheese. Pour water around edges. Cover tightly with foil. Bake 1 hour and 15 minutes or until pasta is tender. Cool 10 minutes before serving.

Makes 6 to 10 servings

SALADS & SIDE DISHES

GAZPACHO SALAD

*This colorful and spicy salad
features the same
combination of tastes and
textures found in the famous
cold Mexican soup. Try it
with freshly toasted Corn
Tortilla Chips (page 32).*

Nutrients per Serving:

Calories	71
(14% of calories from fat)	
Total Fat	1 g
Saturated Fat	<1 g
Cholesterol	0 mg
Sodium	105 mg
Carbohydrate	14 g
Dietary Fiber	3 g
Protein	3 g
Calcium	51 mg
Iron	2 mg
Vitamin A	287 RE
Vitamin C	52 mg

DIETARY EXCHANGES:
3 Vegetable

1½ cups peeled and coarsely chopped tomatoes*
 1 cup peeled, seeded and diced cucumber
 ¾ cup chopped onion
 ½ cup chopped red bell pepper
 ½ cup fresh or frozen corn kernels, cooked and drained
 1 tablespoon lime juice
 1 tablespoon red wine vinegar
 2 teaspoons water
 1 teaspoon extra virgin olive oil
 1 teaspoon minced fresh garlic
 ¼ teaspoon salt
 ¼ teaspoon black pepper
   Pinch ground red pepper
 1 medium head romaine lettuce, torn into bite-sized pieces
 1 cup peeled and diced jicama
 ½ cup fresh cilantro

1 Combine tomatoes, cucumber, onion, bell pepper and corn in large bowl. Combine lime juice, vinegar, water, oil, garlic, salt, black pepper and ground red pepper in small bowl; whisk until well blended. Pour over tomato mixture; toss well. Cover and refrigerate several hours to allow flavors to blend.

2 Toss together lettuce, jicama and cilantro in another large bowl. Divide lettuce mixture evenly among 6 plates. Place ⅔ cup chilled tomato mixture on top of lettuce, spreading to edges.

Makes 6 servings

*To peel tomatoes easily, blanch in boiling water 30 seconds; immediately transfer to bowl of cold water, then peel.

GARDEN GREENS WITH FENNEL DRESSING

The pine nuts add only 1 gram of fat to this salad; however, if you prefer to have only 23% of the calories from fat, omit the nuts. Eating greens is a great, tasty way to get calcium into your diet.

Nutrients per Serving:

Calories	60
(30% of calories from fat)	
Total Fat	2 g
Saturated Fat	<1 g
Cholesterol	0 mg
Sodium	226 mg
Carbohydrate	9 g
Dietary Fiber	1 g
Protein	3 g
Calcium	94 mg
Iron	1 mg
Vitamin A	191 RE
Vitamin C	21 mg

DIETARY EXCHANGES:
1½ Vegetable, ½ Fat

DRESSING

½ teaspoon unflavored gelatin
2 tablespoons cold water
¼ cup boiling water
½ teaspoon salt
½ teaspoon sugar
¼ teaspoon dry mustard
⅛ teaspoon black pepper
¼ teaspoon anise extract *or* ground fennel seeds
1 tablespoon fresh lemon juice
¼ cup raspberry or wine vinegar
1¼ teaspoons walnut or canola oil

SALAD

1 head (10 ounces) Bibb lettuce, torn into bite-sized pieces
1 head (10 ounces) radicchio, torn into bite-sized pieces
1 bunch arugula (3 ounces), torn into bite-sized pieces
1 cup mache *or* spinach leaves, washed and torn into bite-sized pieces
1 fennel bulb (8 ounces), finely chopped (reserve fern for garnish)
1 tablespoon pine nuts, toasted

1 To prepare dressing, sprinkle gelatin over cold water in small bowl; let stand 1 minute to soften. Add boiling water; stir 2 minutes or until gelatin is completely dissolved. Add salt and sugar; stir until sugar is completely dissolved. Add all remaining dressing ingredients except oil; mix well. Slowly whisk in oil until well blended. Cover and refrigerate 2 hours or overnight. Shake well before using.

2 To prepare salad, place all salad ingredients except pine nuts in large bowl. Add dressing; toss until all leaves glisten. Divide salad among 6 chilled salad plates. Top each salad with ½ teaspoon pine nuts. Garnish with sprig of fennel fern, if desired.

Makes 6 servings

GRILLED VEGETABLES

Most vegetables require no preparation before grilling except slicing them into a uniform thickness. However, eggplant is better if sprinkled with a little salt after slicing and drained for an hour before grilling. This removes any bitterness. Not only are grilled vegetables excellent as a side dish, they are also great served over pasta, rice or beans.

¼ cup minced fresh herbs, such as parsley, thyme, rosemary, oregano or basil
1 small eggplant (about ¾ pound), cut into ¼-inch-thick slices
½ teaspoon salt
  Nonstick cooking spray
1 *each* red, green and yellow bell pepper, quartered and seeded
2 zucchini, cut lengthwise into ¼-inch-thick slices
1 fennel bulb, cut lengthwise into ¼-inch-thick slices

1 Combine herbs of your choice in small bowl; let stand 3 hours or overnight.

2 Place eggplant in large colander over bowl; sprinkle with salt. Drain 1 hour.

3 Heat grill until coals are glowing red, but not flaming. Spray vegetables with cooking spray and sprinkle with herb mixture. Grill 10 to 15 minutes or until fork-tender and lightly browned on both sides. (Cooking times vary depending on vegetable; remove vegetables as they are done to avoid overcooking.)

Makes 6 servings

Variation: Cut vegetables into 1-inch cubes and thread onto skewers. Spray with cooking spray and sprinkle with herb mixture. Grill as directed above.

Nutrients per Serving:

Calories	34
(6% of calories from fat)	
Total Fat	<1 g
Saturated Fat	<1 g
Cholesterol	0 mg
Sodium	190 mg
Carbohydrate	8 g
Dietary Fiber	2 g
Protein	1 g
Calcium	24 mg
Iron	1 mg
Vitamin A	54 RE
Vitamin C	43 mg

DIETARY EXCHANGES:
1½ Vegetable

Cook's Tip
Fennel is an anise-flavored, bulb-shaped vegetable with celerylike stems and feathery leaves. Both the base and stems can be eaten raw in salads, grilled or sautéed. The seeds and leaves can be used for seasoning food. Purchase clean, crisp bulbs with no sign of browning.

MARINATED TOMATO SALAD

This uniquely different salad takes full advantage of the colorful array of tomatoes available in the summer. During other seasons, you can make this salad with readily available plum tomatoes. The subtly seasoned marinade enhances the fabulous flavor of truly ripe tomatoes without masking it. This salad should be served at room temperature. Refrigerating tomatoes destroys their natural flavor and texture.

Nutrients per Serving:

Calories	56
(24% of calories from fat)	
Total Fat	2 g
Saturated Fat	<1 g
Cholesterol	0 mg
Sodium	64 mg
Carbohydrate	10 g
Dietary Fiber	2 g
Protein	2 g
Calcium	15 mg
Iron	1 mg
Vitamin A	145 RE
Vitamin C	40 mg

DIETARY EXCHANGES:
2 Vegetable

MARINADE

1½ cups tarragon or white wine vinegar
½ teaspoon salt
¼ cup finely chopped shallots
2 tablespoons finely chopped chives
2 tablespoons fresh lemon juice
¼ teaspoon ground white pepper
2 tablespoons extra virgin olive oil

SALAD

6 plum tomatoes, quartered vertically
2 large yellow tomatoes, sliced horizontally into ½-inch slices
16 red cherry tomatoes, halved vertically
16 small yellow pear tomatoes, halved vertically

1 To prepare marinade, combine vinegar and salt in large bowl; stir until salt is completely dissolved. Add shallots, chives, lemon juice and white pepper; mix well. Slowly whisk in oil until smooth and well blended.

2 Add tomatoes to marinade; toss well. Cover and let stand at room temperature 2 to 3 hours.

3 To serve, place 3 plum tomato quarters on each of 8 salad plates. Add 2 slices yellow tomato, 4 cherry tomato halves and 4 pear tomato halves. Garnish each plate with sunflower sprouts, if desired. (Or, place all marinated tomatoes on large serving plate.)

Makes 8 servings

HONEY GLAZED CARROTS AND PARSNIPS

½ pound carrots, peeled and cut into julienned strips
½ pound parsnips, peeled and cut into julienned strips
¼ cup chopped fresh parsley
2 tablespoons honey

1 Steam carrots and parsnips 3 to 4 minutes until crisp-tender. Rinse under cold running water; drain and set aside.

2 Just before serving, combine carrots, parsnips, parsley and honey in large saucepan or skillet. Cook over medium heat just until heated through. Garnish with fresh Italian parsley, if desired. Serve immediately.   *Makes 6 servings*

Nutrients per Serving:

⅔ cup

Calories	69
(2% of calories from fat)	
Total Fat	<1 g
Saturated Fat	<1 g
Cholesterol	0 mg
Sodium	19 mg
Carbohydrate	17 g
Dietary Fiber	3 g
Protein	1 g
Calcium	28 mg
Iron	1 mg
Vitamin A	1076 RE
Vitamin C	12 mg

DIETARY EXCHANGES:
2½ Vegetable

HERBED GREEN BEANS

1 pound fresh green beans, stem ends removed
1 teaspoon extra virgin olive oil
2 tablespoons chopped fresh basil *or* 2 teaspoons dried basil leaves

1 Steam green beans 5 minutes or until crisp-tender. Rinse under cold running water; drain and set aside.

2 Just before serving, heat oil over medium-low heat in large nonstick skillet. Add basil; cook and stir 1 minute, then add green beans. Cook until heated through. Garnish with additional fresh basil, if desired. Serve immediately.   *Makes 6 servings*

Nutrients per Serving:

⅔ cup

Calories	26
(26% of calories from fat)	
Total Fat	1 g
Saturated Fat	<1 g
Cholesterol	0 mg
Sodium	10 mg
Carbohydrate	5 g
Dietary Fiber	0 g
Protein	1 g
Calcium	35 mg
Iron	1 mg
Vitamin A	39 RE
Vitamin C	6 mg

DIETARY EXCHANGES:
1 Vegetable

PASTA SALAD

Spiral-shaped pastas work best for salads because they hold the dressing well. This vegetable-packed pasta salad is a wonderful side dish for Grilled Marinated Chicken (page 50), but you may easily turn it into an entrée by adding cooked poultry or water-packed canned tuna. For an easy and delicious vegetarian entrée, add your favorite cooked beans.

❖

4 cups broccoli flowerets
2 cups carrot slices
1½ cups chopped tomatoes
½ cup chopped green onions with tops
½ pound spiral pasta, cooked and well drained
1 cup fat free mayonnaise
2 tablespoons white wine vinegar
1 tablespoon extra virgin olive oil
1 tablespoon minced fresh basil *or* 1 teaspoon dried basil leaves
2 teaspoons minced fresh oregano *or* ½ teaspoon dried oregano leaves
1 clove garlic, minced
1 teaspoon sugar
1 teaspoon dry mustard
¼ teaspoon *each* salt and black pepper
½ cup (2 ounces) freshly grated Romano cheese

1 Steam broccoli 3 minutes or until crisp-tender; immediately drain and run under cold water. Steam carrots 4 minutes or until crisp-tender; immediately drain and run under cold water. Combine broccoli, carrots, tomatoes, green onions and pasta in large bowl.

2 Combine all remaining ingredients except cheese in small bowl; blend well. Stir into pasta mixture. Add cheese; toss well. Refrigerate 3 hours or overnight to allow flavors to blend.

Makes 8 servings

Nutrients per Serving:

1¼ cups

Calories	215
(20% of calories from fat)	
Total Fat	5 g
Saturated Fat	2 g
Cholesterol	7 mg
Sodium	573 mg
Carbohydrate	35 g
Dietary Fiber	5 g
Protein	9 g
Calcium	138 mg
Iron	2 mg
Vitamin A	973 RE
Vitamin C	92 mg

DIETARY EXCHANGES:
1½ Starch/Bread,
2½ Vegetable, 1 Fat

STILTON SALAD DRESSING

In this salad dressing, most of the cholesterol usually found in cheese dressings is missing by using tofu for texture and low fat cottage cheese for the lumps associated with the higher fat Stilton. Toasting the walnuts enhances their flavor enormously so that you can use fewer of them. Although adding 1 teaspoon of walnuts to each serving adds 2 grams of fat, it adds a lot of flavor.

Nutrients per Serving:	
Calories	51
(55% of calories from fat)	
Total Fat	3 g
Saturated Fat	2 g
Cholesterol	8 mg
Sodium	265 mg
Carbohydrate	2 g
Dietary Fiber	<1 g
Protein	4 g
Calcium	80 mg
Iron	<1 mg
Vitamin A	23 RE
Vitamin C	1 mg

DIETARY EXCHANGES:
½ Lean Meat, ½ Fat

½ cup buttermilk
¼ cup silken firm tofu
2 ounces Stilton cheese
1 teaspoon fresh lemon juice
1 clove garlic, peeled
¼ teaspoon salt
⅛ teaspoon black pepper
2 tablespoons 1% low fat cottage cheese
   Romaine lettuce hearts, torn into bite-sized pieces (optional)
   Toasted chopped walnuts (optional)

1 Place buttermilk, tofu, Stilton cheese, lemon juice, garlic, salt and black pepper in blender or food processor; process until smooth. Pour mixture into small bowl and fold in cottage cheese. Store in airtight container and refrigerate 3 hours or overnight before serving. Serve with romaine lettuce and toasted walnuts, if desired.

Makes 6 servings

Cook's Tip

To toast walnuts, spread on baking sheet in a single layer. Bake in a preheated 350°F oven 5 to 10 minutes until lightly browned and fragrant. Watch carefully to avoid burning.

DESSERTS

ALMOND BISCOTTI

These no cholesterol, low fat Italian cookies are the perfect guilt free snack to satisfy any sweet tooth.

Nutrients per Serving:

1 biscotti

Calories	56
(21% of calories from fat)	
Total Fat	1 g
Saturated Fat	<1 g
Cholesterol	0 mg
Sodium	53 mg
Carbohydrate	9 g
Dietary Fiber	<1 g
Protein	1 g
Calcium	8 mg
Iron	<1 mg
Vitamin A	9 RE
Vitamin C	<1 mg

DIETARY EXCHANGES:
½ Starch/Bread, ½ Fat

¼ cup finely chopped almonds
½ cup sugar
2 tablespoons margarine
4 egg whites, lightly beaten
2 teaspoons almond extract
2 cups all-purpose flour
2 teaspoons baking powder
¼ teaspoon salt

1 Preheat oven to 375°F. Place almonds in small baking pan. Bake 7 to 8 minutes until golden brown. (Watch carefully to avoid burning.) Set aside.

2 Beat sugar and margarine in medium bowl with electric mixer until smooth. Add egg whites and almond extract; mix well. Combine flour, baking powder and salt in large bowl; mix well. Stir egg white mixture and almonds into flour mixture until well blended.

3 Spray two 9×5-inch loaf pans with nonstick cooking spray. Evenly divide dough between prepared pans. Spread dough evenly over bottoms of pans with wet fingertips. Bake 15 minutes or until knife inserted into centers comes out clean.

4 Remove from oven and turn out onto cutting board. As soon as loaves are cool enough to handle, cut each into 16 (½-inch-thick) slices. Place slices on baking sheets covered with parchment paper or sprayed with cooking spray. Bake 5 minutes; turn over. Bake 5 minutes more or until golden brown. Serve warm *or* cool completely and store in airtight container.

Makes 32 biscotti

MARINATED POACHED PEACHES

*Serve these healthy goodies
whole in dessert bowls
paired with Almond Biscotti
(page 72), or slice and fan
on dessert plates with
Vanilla Sauce (page 84).*

Nutrients per Serving:

1 peach

Calories	83
(2% of calories from fat)	
Total Fat	<1 g
Saturated Fat	<1 g
Cholesterol	0 mg
Sodium	1 mg
Carbohydrate	22 g
Dietary Fiber	1 g
Protein	1 g
Calcium	29 mg
Iron	1 mg
Vitamin A	47 RE
Vitamin C	7 mg

DIETARY EXCHANGES:
1½ Fruit

10 medium peaches
 2 tablespoons whole allspice
10 cinnamon sticks
½ cup sugar

1 Place peaches in large saucepan or stockpot. Cover with water; add allspice and cinnamon. Bring to a boil over high heat. Boil 2 minutes; remove peaches and peel when cool enough to handle. Add sugar to poaching water and boil 5 minutes. Add peaches and simmer 2 minutes more.

2 Remove from heat; cool to room temperature in poaching liquid. Place peaches and liquid in airtight container. Refrigerate 3 hours or overnight. Garnish with fresh mint and raspberries, if desired. Serve cold. *Makes 10 servings*

Cook's Tip
Ripen peaches at room temperature. When ripe, store
in the refrigerator. Peaches are a great source of potassium,
vitamin A and fiber.

HONEY CARROT CAKE

The pineapple in this recipe gives the cake a fabulous flavor and also helps to keep it moist without adding fat. In addition, the frosting contains almost no fat since it is made with Neufchâtel cheese, a lighter version of cream cheese.

Nutrients per Serving:

Calories	272
(29% of calories from fat)	
Total Fat	9 g
Saturated Fat	2 g
Cholesterol	22 mg
Sodium	112 mg
Carbohydrate	45 g
Dietary Fiber	1 g
Protein	4 g
Calcium	42 mg
Iron	1 mg
Vitamin A	623 RE
Vitamin C	3 mg

DIETARY EXCHANGES:
2½ Starch/Bread, ½ Fruit, 1½ Fat

2 cups all-purpose flour
2 teaspoons baking powder
1½ teaspoons ground cinnamon
1 cup firmly packed dark brown sugar
½ cup honey
⅓ cup canola oil
1 whole egg
3 egg whites
3 cups shredded carrots
1 can (8 ounces) crushed pineapple in juice, drained
¼ cup chopped toasted pecans
6 ounces Neufchâtel cheese, softened
¾ cup powdered sugar
1 tablespoon cornstarch
1½ teaspoons vanilla extract

1 Preheat oven to 350°F. Spray 13×9-inch baking pan with nonstick cooking spray; set aside. Combine flour, baking powder and cinnamon in small bowl; set aside. Beat together sugar, honey, oil, whole egg and egg whites in large bowl with electric mixer. Gradually beat flour mixture into sugar mixture on low speed until well blended. Stir in carrots, pineapple and pecans.

2 Pour batter into prepared pan. Bake 40 to 45 minutes until toothpick inserted into center comes out clean. Cool completely in pan on wire rack.

3 To prepare frosting, beat cheese, powdered sugar, cornstarch and vanilla in small bowl until smooth. Spread frosting over top of cake, reserving some frosting to tint with food coloring and pipe carrots for garnish, if desired. Store in refrigerator.

Makes 16 servings

Variation: Instead of folding pecans into batter, sprinkle over frosting for garnish.

FANTASY IN BERRIES

This uniquely different, beautiful and delicious dessert is also very healthy. The berries are high in vitamin C and ricotta cheese is higher in calcium than any other cheese. It is also lots of fun to make. In fact, you may want to put your pastry "cream" in plastic squeeze bottles and let the guests decorate their own "Fantasy."

1 bag (12 ounces) frozen unsweetened raspberries, thawed
¼ cup *plus* 2 tablespoons sugar, divided
1 tablespoon fresh lemon juice
2 cups sliced fresh strawberries
1 cup fresh raspberries
1 cup fresh blueberries
1 cup low fat ricotta cheese
1 teaspoon vanilla extract
¼ teaspoon almond extract

1 To prepare raspberry sauce, place thawed raspberries, ¼ cup sugar and lemon juice in blender or food processor; process until smooth. Pour through strainer to remove seeds.

2 Spoon 3 tablespoons raspberry sauce on each of 8 plates. Tilt each plate, rotating to spread raspberry mixture over bottom of plate.

3 Arrange ¼ cup sliced strawberries, 2 tablespoons fresh raspberries and 2 tablespoons blueberries on top of sauce in desired pattern on each plate.

4 Place cheese, remaining 2 tablespoons sugar, and vanilla and almond extracts in clean blender or food processor; process until smooth and satiny. Spoon cheese mixture into pastry bag and pipe the pastry "cream" onto the berries, using about 2 tablespoons on each serving. (Use star tip to make rosettes or various sizes of writing tips to drizzle "cream" over berries.) Before serving, garnish with mint sprigs and edible flowers, such as pansies, violets or nasturtiums, if desired.

Makes 8 servings

Nutrients per Serving:

Calories	104
(10% of calories from fat)	
Total Fat	1 g
Saturated Fat	<1 g
Cholesterol	4 mg
Sodium	25 mg
Carbohydrate	21 g
Dietary Fiber	5 g
Protein	4 g
Calcium	56 mg
Iron	1 mg
Vitamin A	26 RE
Vitamin C	37 mg

DIETARY EXCHANGES:
½ Lean Meat, 1½ Fruit

FIRE AND ICE

*This whimsical,
southwestern dessert is
designed to represent all of
the colors of the Mexican
flag. It is a perfect finale for
a fiesta and it's fun to
decorate each serving with a
little Mexican flag.*

Nutrients per Serving:

Calories	152
(11% of calories from fat)	
Total Fat	2 g
Saturated Fat	1 g
Cholesterol	7 mg
Sodium	58 mg
Carbohydrate	32 g
Dietary Fiber	3 g
Protein	4 g
Calcium	112 mg
Iron	<1 mg
Vitamin A	32 RE
Vitamin C	62 mg

DIETARY EXCHANGES:
1½ Starch/Bread, 1 Fruit

2 cups vanilla ice milk or low fat ice cream
2 teaspoons finely chopped jalapeño pepper
1 teaspoon grated lime peel, divided
1 cup water
¼ cup sugar
1 cup peeled and chopped kiwifruit
1 tablespoon lime juice
1 cup fresh raspberries

1 Soften ice milk slightly in small bowl. Stir in jalapeño and ½ teaspoon lime peel. Freeze until firm.

2 Combine water, sugar and remaining ½ teaspoon lime peel in small saucepan; bring to a boil. Boil, uncovered, 5 minutes or until reduced by about one-third. Remove from heat and cool to room temperature.

3 Place kiwifruit and lime juice in blender or food processor; process until blended. Stir in water mixture. Pour through fine strainer to remove kiwifruit seeds and lime peel, pressing liquid through strainer with back of spoon. Refrigerate kiwifruit mixture until cold.

4 Pour ¼ cup kiwifruit mixture into each of 6 chilled bowls. Scoop ⅓ cup jalapeño ice milk in center of each bowl. Sprinkle raspberries evenly on top. Garnish with lime peel strips, if desired.

Makes 6 servings

Cook's Tip

Jalapeño peppers can sting and irritate the skin; wear plastic disposable gloves when handling peppers and do not touch eyes. To seed, cut peppers in half lengthwise. Remove seeds, membranes and stems with small paring knife.

TEMPTING APPLE TRIFLES

*Just as Eve tempted Adam
with an apple, you may find
that this scrumptious
dessert is truly the final
touch to winning the lasting
affection of that special
someone in your life...
especially when he or she
learns that there are only
246 calories, 2 grams of fat
and almost no cholesterol
per serving in this
rich-tasting trifle.*

Nutrients per Serving:

Calories	246
(6% of calories from fat)	
Total Fat	2 g
Saturated Fat	<1 g
Cholesterol	1 mg
Sodium	117 mg
Carbohydrate	53 g
Dietary Fiber	2 g
Protein	6 g
Calcium	104 mg
Iron	1 mg
Vitamin A	41 RE
Vitamin C	5 mg

DIETARY EXCHANGES:
2 Starch/Bread, 1½ Fruit

½ cup skim milk
1½ teaspoons cornstarch
4½ teaspoons dark brown sugar
1 egg white
½ teaspoon canola oil
½ teaspoon vanilla extract
½ teaspoon rum extract, divided
¼ cup unsweetened apple cider, divided
2 tablespoons raisins
½ teaspoon ground cinnamon
1 cup peeled and chopped Golden Delicious apple
1 cup ½-inch angel food cake cubes, divided

1 To prepare custard, combine milk and cornstarch in small heavy saucepan; stir until cornstarch is completely dissolved. Add brown sugar, egg white and oil; blend well. Slowly bring to a boil over medium-low heat until thickened, stirring constantly with whisk. Remove from heat; stir in vanilla and ¼ teaspoon rum extract. Set aside; cool completely.

2 Combine 2 tablespoons cider, raisins and cinnamon in medium saucepan; bring to a boil over medium-low heat. Add apple and cook until apple is fork-tender and all liquid has been absorbed, stirring frequently. Remove from heat; set aside to cool.

3 To assemble, place ¼ cup cake cubes in bottom of 2 small trifle or dessert dishes. Combine remaining 2 tablespoons cider and ¼ teaspoon rum extract in small bowl; mix well. Spoon 1½ teaspoons cider mixture over cake in each dish. Spoon ¼ of custard mixture over cake in each dish, then top each with ¼ cup cooked apple mixture. Repeat layers. Serve immediately. Garnish with fresh mint, if desired.

Makes 2 servings

COLD CHERRY MOUSSE WITH VANILLA SAUCE

Nutrients per Serving:

includes 2 tablespoons sauce

Calories	198
(25% of calories from fat)	
Total Fat	6 g
Saturated Fat	1 g
Cholesterol	5 mg
Sodium	64 mg
Carbohydrate	34 g
Dietary Fiber	1 g
Protein	4 g
Calcium	88 mg
Iron	1 mg
Vitamin A	99 RE
Vitamin C	5 mg

DIETARY EXCHANGES:
1½ Starch/Bread, 1 Fruit, 1 Fat

Nutrients per Serving:

1 tablespoon

Calories	25
(21% of calories from fat)	
Total Fat	1 g
Saturated Fat	<1 g
Cholesterol	2 mg
Sodium	12 mg
Carbohydrate	4 g
Dietary Fiber	0 g
Protein	1 g
Calcium	20 mg
Iron	<1 mg
Vitamin A	7 RE
Vitamin C	<1 mg

DIETARY EXCHANGES:
½ Fruit

1 envelope whipped topping mix
½ cup skim milk
½ teaspoon vanilla extract
2 envelopes unflavored gelatin
½ cup sugar
½ cup cold water
1 package (16 ounces) frozen unsweetened cherries, thawed, undrained and divided
1 tablespoon fresh lemon juice
½ teaspoon almond extract
¾ cup Vanilla Sauce (recipe follows)

1 Prepare whipped topping according to package directions using milk and vanilla; set aside. Combine gelatin and sugar in small saucepan; stir in water. Let stand 5 minutes to soften. Heat over low heat until gelatin is completely dissolved. Cool to room temperature.

2 Set aside 1 cup cherries without juice for garnish. Place remaining cherries and juice in blender. Add lemon juice, almond extract and gelatin mixture; process until blended. Fold cherry purée into whipped topping until no streaks of white show. Pour mixture into Bundt pan or ring mold. Refrigerate 4 hours or overnight until jelled.

3 To serve, unmold mousse onto large serving plate. Spoon remaining 1 cup cherries into center of mousse. Serve with Vanilla Sauce. Garnish with fresh mint, if desired.

Makes 6 servings

VANILLA SAUCE

4½ teaspoons cherry brandy *or* 1 teaspoon vanilla extract plus ½ teaspoon cherry extract
¾ cup melted vanilla ice milk or low fat ice cream, cooled

1 Stir brandy into ice milk in small bowl; blend well. *Makes 12 servings*

Variations: You may vary the flavor just by trying different liqueurs or extracts. Try Grand Marnier in the sauce and pour over fresh berries. Amaretto in the sauce tastes great over sliced peaches. Add dark rum to the sauce and serve over sliced bananas.

FRESH APRICOT COBBLER

1 cup all-purpose flour
¼ cup granulated sugar
2 tablespoons instant nonfat dry milk powder
2 teaspoons baking powder
¼ teaspoon baking soda
¼ teaspoon salt
2 tablespoons canola oil
7 tablespoons buttermilk
½ cup firmly packed dark brown sugar
4½ teaspoons cornstarch
½ cup water
1½ pounds ripe apricots, pits removed, quartered
   Cinnamon Yogurt Topping (page 88)

1 Preheat oven to 400°F. Combine flour, granulated sugar, dry milk, baking powder, baking soda and salt in medium bowl. Stir in oil until mixture becomes crumbly. Add buttermilk and stir just until moistened.

2 Combine brown sugar, cornstarch and water in medium saucepan, stirring until cornstarch is dissolved. Cook over medium heat until thickened, stirring constantly. Add apricots; cook and stir about 3 minutes or until apricots are completely covered in sauce.

3 Pour into 8-inch square baking pan and immediately drop flour mixture in small spoonfuls on top of apricot mixture. Bake 25 minutes or until topping is lightly browned. Serve warm with Cinnamon Yogurt Topping, if desired.   *Makes 6 servings*

Nutrients per Serving:

without yogurt topping

Calories	293
(16% of calories from fat)	
Total Fat	5 g
Saturated Fat	1 g
Cholesterol	1 mg
Sodium	286 mg
Carbohydrate	58 g
Dietary Fiber	3 g
Protein	5 g
Calcium	93 mg
Iron	2 mg
Vitamin A	308 RE
Vitamin C	12 mg

DIETARY EXCHANGES:
2½ Starch/Bread, 1 Fruit, 1 Fat

Nutrients per Serving:

with ½ cup yogurt topping

Calories	364
(13% of calories from fat)	
Total Fat	5 g
Saturated Fat	1 g
Cholesterol	2 mg
Sodium	332 mg
Carbohydrate	72 g
Dietary Fiber	3 g
Protein	9 g
Calcium	205 mg
Iron	2 mg
Vitamin A	329 RE
Vitamin C	13 mg

DIETARY EXCHANGES:
3 Starch/Bread, ½ Milk, 1 Fruit, 1 Fat

CINNAMON YOGURT TOPPPING

This melt-in-your-mouth dessert can certainly stand alone, but a dollop of it is fantastic on Fresh Apricot Cobbler (page 86). Because this yogurt has not actually been frozen and processed, all of its valuable bacteria are still active. It is best served soon after it is made. Recipe pictured on page 87.

1 envelope unflavored gelatin
2 tablespoons cold water
¼ cup boiling water
1 cup plain nonfat yogurt
¼ cup instant nonfat dry milk powder
¼ cup sugar
¼ to ½ teaspoon ground cinnamon
1½ teaspoons vanilla extract
2 cups crushed ice

1 Sprinkle gelatin over cold water in medium bowl; let stand 1 minute to soften. Add boiling water; stir about 2 minutes or until gelatin is completely dissolved. Add yogurt and mix well. Refrigerate until jelled.

2 Place yogurt mixture in blender or food processor. Add all remaining ingredients; process until smooth. Serve immediately or cover and refrigerate.

Makes 6 servings

Nutrients per Serving:

½ cup

Calories	72
(1% of calories from fat)	
Total Fat	<1 g
Saturated Fat	<1 g
Cholesterol	1 mg
Sodium	46 mg
Carbohydrate	13 g
Dietary Fiber	0 g
Protein	4 g
Calcium	113 mg
Iron	<1 mg
Vitamin A	21 RE
Vitamin C	1 mg

DIETARY EXCHANGES:
½ Starch/Bread, ½ Milk

Health Note

Apricots are a super source of beta carotene. Research continues to show that antioxidants, such as beta carotene, have a disease-fighting role. Try dried apricots for a wonderful, quick snack to help increase your beta carotene intake.

A Message from Jeanne Jones

Most people are well aware of the importance of good nutrition and follow all of the basic guidelines—until they entertain! Then they pull out all the stops because they are afraid of not impressing their company with their culinary capabilities. They pass high fat hors d'oeuvres. The salad gets a thick, creamy dressing. The usually broiled fish, poultry or meat gets cooked in a rich sauce, and the steamed vegetables get coated with melted butter. The truth of the matter is that almost all of us would be much happier with a lighter, lower fat menu when we are guests.

The next time you are planning a party menu, pretend that you are going to be the guest. You will be amazed at the difference it makes in your menu selections and at how appreciative your guests will be. To help you get started, you will find nine complete party menus (see page 90) in this book ranging from an "Easy Make-Ahead Casual Party" menu to a "Formal Dinner Party." There is also a selection of light hors d'oeuvres for a "Cocktail Buffet" and a delightfully different "Sunday Brunch."

Giving a party can be lots of fun, rather than just lots of work, if you plan ahead properly. It is practically impossible to plan a menu, do the shopping and cooking, and give the party all on the same day. A good rule of thumb in party planning, whether it is a formal dinner or backyard barbecue, is to plan your menu at least two days before the party and do most of your shopping that day. Last minute shopping should be limited to only perishable ingredients, such as seafood and some fruits and vegetables. Prepare as many dishes as possible the day before your party, leaving only those dishes requiring last minute preparation.

Your personal style is what makes your parties special. It doesn't matter how large or small your home is, using the space you have in innovative ways is what is important. You don't have to rent a room or borrow china, crystal and silver in order to have a successful party. Just mix and match whatever you have and give your parties your own individual touch.

We all consider an invitation for a meal in someone's home the ultimate compliment. Why not pay this compliment to your family and friends as often as you can? You will find it to be both rewarding and lots of fun.

Jeanne Jones

Jeanne Jones
Internationally Syndicated Food Columnist

MENU IDEAS

SUNDAY BRUNCH *(For Four)*

Minted Melon Soup (page 28)
Eggs Primavera (page 48)
Whole Wheat Herb Bread (page 36)
Apricot Butter (page 36)
Spiced Apple Tea (page 32)

SUMMER HARVEST MENU *(For Six)*

Corn and Tomato Chowder (page 16)
Garden Greens with Fennel Dressing (page 60)
Vegetable Risotto (page 42)
Fresh Apricot Cobbler (page 86)
Cinnamon Yogurt Topping (page 88)

BRIDAL SHOWER *(For Eight)*

Marinated Tomato Salad (page 64)
Cheddar Cheese Strata (page 52)
Miniature Fruit Muffins (page 34)
Fantasy in Berries (page 78)

ROMANTIC DINNER *(For Two)*

Cold Asparagus with Lemon-Mustard Dressing (page 24)
Salmon en Papillote (page 44)
Tempting Apple Trifles (page 82)

EASY MAKE-AHEAD CASUAL PARTY *(For Six)*

Gazpacho Salad (page 58)
Corn Tortilla Chips (page 32)
Southwestern Beef and Bean Lasagna (page 56)
Fire and Ice (page 80)

COCKTAIL BUFFET *(For Eight)*

Petite Pizzas (page 18)
Polenta Triangles (page 30)
Crostini (page 10)
Tiny Seafood Tostadas with Black Bean Dip (page 26)
Black Bean Dip (page 26) with Corn Tortilla Chips (page 32)
Gingered Chicken Pot Stickers (page 22)
Citrus Cooler (page 20)
Chilled Champagne

FORMAL DINNER PARTY *(For Six)*

Marinated Artichokes & Shrimp in Citrus Vinaigrette (page 12)
Rack of Lamb with Dijon-Mustard Sauce (page 47)
Rosemary Bread Sticks (page 40)
Honey Glazed Carrots and Parsnips (page 66)
Herbed Green Beans (page 66)
Stilton Salad Dressing (page 70) over Romaine Lettuce
Red Wine or Sparkling Water
Cold Cherry Mousse with Vanilla Sauce (page 84)
Fresh Brewed Coffee

FAMILY REUNION *(For Eight)*

(All recipes may be doubled for 16)
Pasta Salad (page 68)
Grilled Marinated Chicken (page 50)
Garlic Bread (page 39)
Grilled Vegetables (page 62)
Cold Lemonade
Honey Carrot Cake (page 76)
Basket of Fresh Fruits

TASTE OF THE MEDITERRANEAN *(For Ten)*

Roasted Eggplant Spread with Focaccia (page 14)
Seafood Paella (page 54)
Marinated Poached Peaches (page 74)
Almond Biscotti (page 72)
Espresso Coffee

*Personalized Nutrition Reference for Different Calorie Levels**

Daily Calorie Level	1,600	2,000	2,200	2,800
Total Fat	53 g	65 g	73 g	93 g
% of Calories from Fat	30%	30%	30%	30%
Saturated Fat	18 g	20 g	24 g	31 g
Carbohydrate	240 g	300 g	330 g	420 g
Protein	46 g**	50 g	55 g	70 g
Dietary Fiber	20 g***	25 g	25 g	32 g
Cholesterol	300 mg	300 mg	300 mg	300 mg
Sodium	2,400 mg	2,400 mg	2,400 mg	2,400 mg
Calcium	1,000 mg	1,000 mg	1,000 mg	1,000 mg
Iron	18 mg	18 mg	18 mg	18 mg
Vitamin A	1,000 RE	1,000 RE	1,000 RE	1,000 RE
Vitamin C	60 mg	60 mg	60 mg	60 mg

  * Numbers may be rounded
 ** 46 g is the minimum amount of protein recommended for all
    calorie levels below 1,800.
*** 20 g is the minimum amount of fiber recommended for all calorie
    levels below 2,000.

Note: These calorie levels may not apply to children or adolescents, who have
varying calorie requirements. For specific advice concerning calorie levels,
please consult a registered dietitian, qualified health professional or pediatrician.

VOLUME MEASUREMENTS (dry)

1/8 teaspoon = 0.5 mL
1/4 teaspoon = 1 mL
1/2 teaspoon = 2 mL
3/4 teaspoon = 4 mL
1 teaspoon = 5 mL
1 tablespoon = 15 mL
2 tablespoons = 30 mL
1/4 cup = 60 mL
1/3 cup = 75 mL
1/2 cup = 125 mL
2/3 cup = 150 mL
3/4 cup = 175 mL
1 cup = 250 mL
2 cups = 1 pint = 500 mL
3 cups = 750 mL
4 cups = 1 quart = 1 L

VOLUME MEASUREMENTS (fluid)

1 fluid ounce (2 tablespoons) = 30 mL
4 fluid ounces (1/2 cup) = 125 mL
8 fluid ounces (1 cup) = 250 mL
12 fluid ounces (1 1/2 cups) = 375 mL
16 fluid ounces (2 cups) = 500 mL

WEIGHTS (mass)

1/2 ounce = 15 g
1 ounce = 30 g
3 ounces = 90 g
4 ounces = 120 g
8 ounces = 225 g
10 ounces = 285 g
12 ounces = 360 g
16 ounces = 1 pound = 450 g

DIMENSIONS

1/16 inch = 2 mm
1/8 inch = 3 mm
1/4 inch = 6 mm
1/2 inch = 1.5 cm
3/4 inch = 2 cm
1 inch = 2.5 cm

OVEN TEMPERATURES

250°F = 120°C
275°F = 140°C
300°F = 150°C
325°F = 160°C
350°F = 180°C
375°F = 190°C
400°F = 200°C
425°F = 220°C
450°F = 230°C

BAKING PAN SIZES

Utensil	Size in Inches/Quarts	Metric Volume	Size in Centimeters
Baking or Cake Pan (square or rectangular)	8×8×2	2 L	20×20×5
	9×9×2	2.5 L	22×22×5
	12×8×2	3 L	30×20×5
	13×9×2	3.5 L	33×23×5
Loaf Pan	8×4×3	1.5 L	20×10×7
	9×5×3	2 L	23×13×7
Round Layer Cake Pan	8×1½	1.2 L	20×4
	9×1½	1.5 L	23×4
Pie Plate	8×1¼	750 mL	20×3
	9×1¼	1 L	23×3
Baking Dish or Casserole	1 quart	1 L	—
	1½ quart	1.5 L	—
	2 quart	2 L	—